Table of Contents

Section	Page

List of Figures

List of Tables

I. Introduction

"A new scientific truth does not triumph by convincing its opponents and making them see the light, but rather because its opponents eventually die, and a new generation grows up that is familiar with it."
- *Max Planck*

Background and Problem Statement

This study polls and evaluates the opinions of a panel of subject matter experts and senior military leaders with respect to the concept of merging air-refueling (AR) capability with Remotely Piloted Aircraft (RPA) technology. This conceptualization results in several different scenarios. First, the existing manned tanker fleet could air-refuel RPAs: this concept has already been developed through the F/A-18 Automated Air Refueling (AAR) project carried out by the National Aeronautics and Space Administration (NASA). Second, unmanned aircraft could be created to air-refuel our existing manned receiver aircraft; this idea has yet to be considered or accepted for further development. The third scenario, and the one that this research focuses on, consists of unmanned tanker aircraft conducting AR against unmanned receiver aircraft.

Procurement of the current tanker fleet has occurred in a strikingly similar fashion for each platform: the Boeing 707 became the KC-135, the McDonnell Douglas DC-10 became the KC-10, and more recently, the Boeing 767 has now become the KC-46. In essence, procurement of tankers has followed a model of retrofitting an existing airframe for the purpose of the AR mission. Currently, RPAs have emerged as one of the most "in demand" capabilities the United States Air Force (USAF) provides to the Joint Force. The intersection of AR capability with RPA technology could revolutionize force extension as we know it. The need for this marriage has been identified in several official USAF documents, yet, to date, there has been little coordinated policy action on the topic. This lack has reached a critical point, as the number of RPAs in our fleet grows and future Joint policy calls for the ability to sustain unmanned airborne forces over greater and greater ranges.

As a born and bred tanker pilot, the air-refueling mission is near and dear to my heart. Furthermore, I have witnessed first-hand the cultural aversion towards RPAs within the pilot community, along with the ensuing detrimental effects of this mindset. The proposal to gauge the attitudes and experiences of experts and senior leaders (SL) in this area points to approaches to overcome the remaining cultural impediments and to shift paradigms. Our Air Force (AF) requires both the capability and the willingness to meet future customer demands with respect to RPAs. As such, the following statement outlines the problem:

> *RPAs are growing both in number of platforms and importance to the USAF operational mission. The ability to refuel these platforms in the air could well be a game-changer. The purpose of this study is to acquire insight and recommendations from subject matter experts and senior military leaders on options and methodology to procure this capability.*

Research Question

The study research question thus follows:

What policy, programming, and procurement issues must be addressed to enable the capability of USAF-provided RPA tankers to air-refuel receiver RPA customers?

Research Objectives and Focus

The issue of force extending our nation's RPAs demands our AF's immediate attention. This study specifically addresses the use of RPAs as tankers to air-refuel receiver RPAs. A specialized application of this concept is the topic of air-refueling the Navy's Unmanned Carrier Launched Airborne Surveillance and Strike (N-UCLASS). This system is a key element of the AirSea Battle Concept (ASBC) signed by the Secretary of the Air Force (SECAF) and Secretary of the Navy (SECNAV) during the summer of 2011. The purpose of the ASBC is to address the vast distances of the Pacific theater that would have to be overcome in a conflict with China. Specifically, it identifies a requirement to air-refuel the N-UCLASS in response to a broad need for increased carrier aircraft range (Ehrhard and Work, 2008). The N-UCLASS story, which is further analyzed in the literature review of this manuscript, is a prime application of the concepts this study endeavors to unravel. Due to non-disclosure agreements, however, the scope of this study remained broad in order to examine the unmanned air-refueling of RPAs in general, thus enabling greater applicability of the results. Hence, the goal of this research was to gather opinions, acknowledge differences, and bring to light consensus on how the USAF should proceed in filling the capability gap that air-refueling RPAs poses. The aim was to generate a dialogue that initiated clear articulation of future requirements.

Methodology: The Delphi Study

The Delphi methodology is an appropriate instrument for this research. It allows the researcher to act as a facilitator in generating a dialog. It is an iterative approach in which the researcher begins with open-ended questions intended to generate ideas. These ideas are fed back, anonymously, to the participants who then hone and focus their subsequent inputs. Ultimately, the goal is to converge on the final answer.

This particular study was accomplished through a three-round Delphi study using a panel of experts in the field, along with a separate, stand-alone round that targeted senior military leaders. The following five research questions formed the basis of this Delphi study (Table 1):

Table 1. Delphi Research Questions

1) Which RPA in the current AF inventory could be used to air-refuel future RPAs without major structural changes to the aircraft?
2) What are the advantages to be gained over manned AR platforms, including new mission sets that could be created, by utilizing RPAs as tankers to air-refuel receiver RPAs?
3) What are the unavoidable drawbacks of utilizing RPAs to air refuel receiver RPAs?
4) What difficulties need to be addressed early in prototyping, planning, procurement, or training in order to successfully utilize RPAs as tankers to air-refuel receiver RPAs?
5) What paradigm shifts from our current AR methods must occur to best incorporate the concept of using RPAs as tankers to air-refuel receiver RPAs, considering sound systems engineering techniques as well as the future anti-access / area denial (A2/AD) needs of tomorrow's conflicts?

The first round consisted of the five open-ended questions shown above and was intended to generate ideas. In essence, Round One was a brainstorming session free from the vagaries of groupthink. Round Two was produced based on the ideas gleaned from participant responses in round one. It allowed the expert panel to rate the ideas generated by the entire panel for each question. Finally, in Round Three, consensus and non-consensus ideas were revealed to the panel, along with any comments provided by individual members. The participants were then given the opportunity to change their responses based on the group's statistics and the comments provided. The stand-alone round targeting senior military leaders was identical to Round Two for the expert panel. The intent was to draw-in SL input while minimizing the time required, thereby boosting participation.

4

Benefits and Implications of the Research

The primary benefit of this research is to serve as an impetus for further development of RPA AR capability. I was able to stimulate discussion among experts, engage and educate SL on the subject, and ultimately reveal an initial consensus for future policy requirements. Additionally, the results are specifically applicable to the capability gap that the N-UCLASS presents, identifying actions the AF ought to heed in satisfying its customer's needs.

II. Literature Review

"Those who cannot remember the past are condemned to repeat it."
- *George Santayana*

This section serves as a call to action for USAF service providers of AR to initiate coordination and cooperation with stakeholders to define future requirements for RPAs performing the AR mission. The literature review begins with an affirmation of the vital role AR has played in warfare throughout its distinguished history. Next is an examination of the stunted implementation RPAs have experienced throughout their existence. The following section outlines the progress made thus far in the marriage of the AR mission with RPA technology. Finally, a specific capability gap is indentified in the N-UCLASS, particularly in light of the ASBC whose purpose is to address the growing Anti-Access / Area Denial (A2/AD) challenges in the Pacific theater of operations. Ultimately, it is the duty of the USAF to fulfill this customer requirement to the utmost of the service's ability!

History of Air Refueling and its Doctrine

Dougherty (1996) asserts that no aircraft in the USAF inventory is capable of responsive global power projection without AR; quite simply, tankers are the cornerstone of "Global Reach – Global Power!" According to the Office of the Historian at Headquarters Strategic Air Command (1990), the history of AR began in 1918 when Lieutenant Godfrey L. Cabot, a USN Reserve pilot, began snaring cans of gasoline positioned on floats. This undertaking was designed as a test of the feasibility of putting fuel on ships in such a way that aircraft could grab it and refuel in-flight on transatlantic flights. On 2 October 1921, rudimentary flight refueling was demonstrated in

Washington DC when a USN Lieutenant in the rear cockpit of a Huff-Daland HD-4 aircraft used a grappling hook to snatch a five-gallon can of gasoline from a float in the Potomac River. A Long Beach "publicity stunt" marked the first true "air-to-air" refueling on record when Wesley May, a wing walker with a five-gallon can of gasoline strapped to his back, climbed from a Lincoln Standard onto a JN-4, then poured the gasoline into the tank of the second aircraft. In April of 1923, two United States Army Air Service (USAAS) de Havilland DH-4Bs demonstrated the feasibility of transferring fuel between aircraft by performing the first in-flight hose contact, all under the direction of then-Major Henry H. "Hap" Arnold. Later that year, the USAAS conducted its first successful AR, and Captain Lowell H. Smith, along with Lieutenant John P. Richter, set new marks for duration and distance, culminating in one flight of over 37 hours, made possible through 15 hose contacts. In January of 1929, the flight of the "Question Mark" established the practical value of AR and tested crew and aircraft endurance. Commanded by then-Major Carl A. Spaatz, the modified Atlantic (Fokker) C-2A remained airborne for an astonishing six-plus days, until engine problems forced it to land. Two modified Douglas C-1 biplanes played the role of tankers, passing 5,700 gallons of fuel, as well as oil, food and water to the receiver aircraft over the course of 37 hookups (HQ SAC, 1990). Spaatz, who later became the first Air Force Chief of Staff (AFCoS), proposed that all future aircraft acquisitions be equipped for AR during manufacture (Dougherty, 1996).

Spaatz was not alone in his unwavering support for the development of AR capability. The Italian air power theorist, Giulio Douhet, believed that range was the defining characteristic distinguishing air power from land or sea power; in his eyes, extended range equated to strategic effect. During his tenure as AFCoS (1948-1953), General Hoyt S. Vandenberg, also directed that all future tactical aircraft be AR-capable (Dougherty, 1996). Further, Major General Perry B. Griffith (1960:12) asserted that "No single innovation of recent times has contributed more to air power flexibility than the aerial tanker." General Curtis E. LeMay was also such a staunch proponent of AR that he stated: "If you give us more money for jet airplanes, I would buy tankers, not airplanes for MATS [Military Air transport Service, ancestor of AMC]...I think we would increase our combat capability more in that manner" (Basom, 2007:7).

Dougherty (1996) affirms that AR still serves as a force multiplier by increasing the speed, range, lethality, flexibility and versatility of today's airborne weapon systems through the extension of aircraft range to the limit of the aircrew.

Hence, in 1948 Boeing proposed the flying boom concept and shortly thereafter, Strategic Air Command (SAC) procured the KC-97

Next came the DASH-80 in 1954, and finally, in 1957, the first of a generation of tankers still in use today, the KC-135A. Figure 2 is a depiction of the infamous tanker barrel roll, showing the wing inverted with the engines balanced precariously on top. Rumor has it that this particular demonstration was the impetus for proceeding with the purchase of the Boeing 707; not the most objective or systems engineering oriented approach to procurement that we try to adhere to today!

AR alleviated the significant shortfall of strategic airlift's dependence on en-route basing, dramatically increasing airlift effectiveness and efficiency. The tanker bridge for

Somalia in 1993 that extended nearly half way around the world demonstrated for all that AR was a greater force multiplier than previously realized. In 1991 during Desert Storm, tankers increased both the speed and the mass of attacks as well as provided a vital margin of safety. US Central Command Air Forces (CENTAF) officials hailed that the air campaign was heavily tanker dependent and that "...tankers were the most critical limitations" (Dougherty, 1996:36).

The Joint Air Power Competence Centre (JAPCC) provided vital insight into the international perspective on the role of AR. According to the North Atlantic Treaty Organization (NATO), the primary AR effect is "spatial or temporal extension of other air capabilities by providing additional fuel to airborne aircraft" (JAPCC, 2007:2). Second order effects of this extension include enhanced flexibility, reduced operating locations, and increased payload capacity. Further, the JAPCC identified the relevant measures of merit for the effect as the right amount at the right time in the right place, in addition to reliability. Ultimately, AR is viewed by the JAPCC as an enabling or supporting effect that is instrumental to accomplishing ultimate air effects (JAPCC, 2007).

Despite the proven significance of air refueling in doctrine, the more recent tanker procurement process has been wrought with controversy and the acquisition process not reflective of its importance. As Mazzara (2009) points out, despite its critical importance to air power, AR technology has evolved little in the last 50 years; the AF still uses the same basic refueling systems designed for SAC over half a century ago. Moreover, procurement of the current tanker fleet has occurred in a strikingly similar fashion for each platform: the Boeing 707 became the KC-135, the McDonnell Douglas DC-10 became the KC-10, and most recently, the Boeing 767 was finally identified to become the KC-46. In essence, the procurement of tankers has followed a model of retrofitting an existing airframe for the purpose of the AR mission. Basom (2007) points out that an enormous advantage of proceeding in this fashion is the cost savings reaped from previous civilian research and development efforts. He goes on to say that an additional advantage is the time compression from design, flight testing and operational delivery since the basic airframe has already received its airworthiness certificate and only requires minor testing of the added AR systems (Basom, 2007).

On the other hand, the procurement process used thus far contradicts the very fundamentals of good systems engineering. According to the International Council on Systems Engineering (INCOSE) (2004), systems engineering is an interdisciplinary approach and a means to enable the realization of successful systems. This end goal is accomplished through defining customer needs and required functionality early in the development cycle, documenting requirements, and then proceeding with design synthesis and system validation while considering the complete problem. It integrates all the disciplines and specialty groups into a team effort, forming a structured development process that proceeds from concept to production to operation. Finally, it considers both the business and the technical needs of all customers with a goal of providing a quality product that meets the user needs (INCOSE, 2004). Thus, with respect to the field of AR, a good systems engineering approach would suggest that all stakeholders come together to identify capability gaps which the USAF as the service provider then seeks to fill for the customer.

A final point on the evolutionary progression of AR is the US's enjoyment of a sheer monopoly on AR assets since its very inception. The USAF's fleet of tankers consists of 59 KC-10s and 414 KC-135s (AMMP, 2012), well over and above that of any other nation in the world. Hence the USAF is the primary provider worldwide to USAF, USN and Marine receiver customers, as well as to our coalition and NATO partners with a need for tanker support. This particular point may contribute to the US military's complacency in the technological and conceptual advancement of this critical mission set.

Evolution of Remotely Piloted Aircraft

While the following picture (Figure 3) is nothing more than a satirical cartoon, it adeptly portrays the idea of conducting reconnaissance from afar via an aerial vehicle; in fact spying from the vantage point of a kite is the earliest known form of this capability.

According to Mets (2010), the idea of striking or spying from afar with unmanned systems is older than most think. As far back as 200 BC, the Chinese used kites to observe the extent of enemy fortifications and to fly noise devices over enemy camps as distractions. In the Spanish-American War, a photographer flew a camera on a kite to obtain aerial pictures of the conflict. The Army's principal unmanned effort in World War I (WWI) consisted of the Kettering Bug shown Figure 4; Orville Wright and Henry H. "Hap" Arnold were among those involved in the effort to operate the vehicles that were autonomous once launched.

Unfortunately, this endeavor ran out of steam following the Armistice. During World War II (WWII), the Japanese released thousands of unmanned balloons built by school children and operated by the military to reach the American homeland; while most of them were lost or shot down, one was actually successful in causing six American fatalities (Mets, 2010).

In contrast to the distinguished history of AR, the more recent evolution of RPAs has consistently fought an uphill battle for acceptance. Singer (2011) asserts that while science fiction directly inspired many of the weapons we now use, military robotics actually has quite a lengthy history, and as Mets (2010) points out, RPAs developed in a way similar to early aircraft, being used first for reconnaissance and surveillance. According to Singer (2011), the first mass-produced unmanned plane in history emerged from a true Hollywood heritage. WWI British flyer Reginald Denny, who became a postwar stunt pilot and hobbyist of radio-controlled model airplanes, pitched his RP-4 "Dennymite" to the Army as a target drone for anti-aircraft gunners in the late 1930s. Initially, the Army only ordered 53, redesignating it as the OQ-1. Immediately following the attack on Pearl Harbor though, an urgent need for anti-aircraft gunners – and target drones – drove the US military to buy nearly 15,000 Dennymites. The Germans were the first to deploy remotely piloted aerial drones, as opposed to simply pre-programmed vehicles. In 1944 the US's focus on aerial weapons led the USAAF and USN to launch Operations Aphrodite and Anvil. In this next step towards unmanned flight, a crew would get an airplane airborne, arm the explosives and then bail-out, allowing a nearby mother-ship to take remote control and steer the plane into targets too well protected for manned bombers to risk approaching (Singer, 2011).

One of the most influential documents of the time was a report to General of the Army, Henry H. "Hap" Arnold which was submitted on behalf of the Army Air Force (AAF) Scientific Advisory Group by Theodor Von Karman. This work, titled "Toward New Horizons" was declassified in 1945. In it, Von Karman and his associates make several recommendations based on the General's questions, as well as the current and future state of affairs, as they viewed it at the time. Von Karman (1945) first delineated several assumptions, some of which are strikingly applicable still today. He asserted that US prewar research and development has often been inferior to our enemies. Further, one of the fundamental principles of American democracy is that personnel casualties are distasteful. Additionally, he posited that our country will not support a large standing Army. Finally, he maintained that while the AAF at the time received 43% of current War Department appropriations, he predicted that this level of allotment may not continue (Von Karman, 1945). These points all align with the challenges facing our military today in the form of shrinking budgets and downsizing of the force. Thus, he proposed several questions to guide his group's research, with the following among them: "Is it not possible to determine if another totally different weapon will replace the airplane? Are manless remote-controlled radar or television assisted precision military rockets or multiple purpose seekers a possibility?" (Von Karman, 1945:3)

The study resulted in a plethora of recommendations, several dealing directly with unmanned flight. Von Karman decreed that principal goals over the next ten years ought to include the development of pilotless aircraft, and remote-controlled / automatic fighter and bomber forces. Alongside these developments, a global strategy for application of this capability should be fleshed out, to include a properly distributed network of bases

15

within and beyond the limits of the continental US. He further claimed that research problems should be considered in their relation to the functions of the AF, rather than as isolated scientific problems. As such, he called for the establishment of development centers for making the novel methods suggested by scientific discovery practical; development centers established for definite tasks are more efficient than separate laboratories for isolated branches of science. Ultimately, he called for a proper balance between weapons directed by humans, assisted by electronic devices, and purely automatic weapons to be established (Von Karman, 1945). His recommendations incorporate several common themes we strive for today: proper system's engineering, business process improvement, and breaking down stovepipes.

Despite Von Karman's counsel, Singer (2011) observed that the evolution of remotely operated weapons, including aircraft, slowed considerably following WWII. In fact, the newly independent USAF actually frowned on unmanned aircraft as a professional threat. Thus, the Pentagon left further development of such systems to the US Army and the USN. In 1962, however, Ryan Aeronautical was awarded a substantial military contract to manufacture an unmanned reconnaissance aircraft coined the Model 147 Lightning Bug shown in Figure 5.

Its many high- and low- altitude variants flew over 3,400 missions over Southeast Asia from 1962 to 1975, but because the uses of such unmanned systems were mostly classified, there was little public knowledge of their relative success, hence little impetus to solve the problems they encountered (Singer, 2011). The next major US military contract toward unmanned aircraft occurred in 1979 with the Lockheed MGM-105 Aquila program. Due to the late addition of a plethora of new requirements, the budget mounted and the program was eventually canceled. Thus, as Singer (2011) stresses, the cause of unmanned vehicles was set further back more by policy decisions than by a dearth of technology.

Mets (2010) asserted that RPAs fell into the doldrums during the post Vietnam drawdown. J.R. Wilson jokingly wrote in Aerospace America, "[Unmanned aircraft] are the vampires of military acquisitions—rising up every few years since WWII, only to be buried until the next decade brings them a shot at new life" (Wilson, 2007:28). The USAF has been criticized for allowing RPA development to lag after Vietnam, however, there were several technological and economical obstacles that had to be overcome. For one, as long as RPAs had to be carried under the wings of C-130s, the RPAs wingspan was limited, reducing its endurance capabilities. Also, the logistical footprint of deploying the RPA included that of its mother-ship, the C-130.

Although the US debuted such smart weapons as precision guided bombs with great success in the 1991 Persian Gulf War, unmanned systems didn't play a major role. One exception was the USN's use of the Israeli developed Pioneer drone, an unmanned plane similar to the Aquila; during one mission, a Pioneer overflew a group of Iraqi soldiers who promptly waved white flags at the drone, the first time in history that human soldiers surrendered to an unmanned system! According to Thompson (2000), the initial prompt for the Department of Defense (DoD) to begin actively pursuing US built RPA systems stemmed from Israeli RPA combat success as well as the remarkable performance of the Israeli built Pioneer RPA flown by the US military in Desert Storm.

Carmichael, Devine, and Kaufman (1996) avowed that there still remained a reconnaissance gap at the time that senior officials wanted to fill. Singer (2011) identified the 1995 integration of the Global Positioning System (GPS) as what one USAF officer called a "magic moment" in RPA history. Mets (2010) noted that the installation of GPS allowed for liberation from navigation assistance from a mother-ship and, more importantly, reduced costs through runway recovery. He further asserted, however, that the growing interest by Soldiers combined with apparent disinterest among

Airmen tended to reinforce ancient rivalries between the services. In fact, during its early days, the Predator program actually belonged to the Army (Mets, 2010). The next major milestone then, occurred in 1996 when the USAF began its first RPA operations squadron near Las Vegas, Nevada, flying the medium-altitude Predator surveillance and reconnaissance platform (Thompson, 2000). Note that this breakthrough occurred over 50 years after Von Karman first recommended it!

The propeller driven Predator completed over 350 missions in support of Operation Joint Endeavor in Bosnia. This success provided the momentum for development of a jet propelled RPA capable of flying at higher altitudes and equipped with advanced Intelligence, Surveillance, and Reconnaissance (ISR) equipment. Thus, the RQ-4 Global Hawk was born. Despite flying only 5% of the Operation Iraqi Freedom sorties, the Global Hawk accounted for over 55% of time sensitive targeting against enemy air defense assets. Its achievements were lauded by General Tommy Franks, Commander, US Central Command (CENTCOM) in 2002 when he enumerated the following:

> Global Hawk unmanned aerial vehicles have been proven to be invaluable in providing long dwell surveillance, tracking, positive identification, and collateral and strike damage assessment. Global Hawk, for example, flew sorties approaching 30 hours in duration and imaged over 600 targets during a single mission over Afghanistan (Department of the Air Force, 2005).

Figure 6 shows how flight hours have nearly doubled each year for large RPAs from 1996 to 2010.

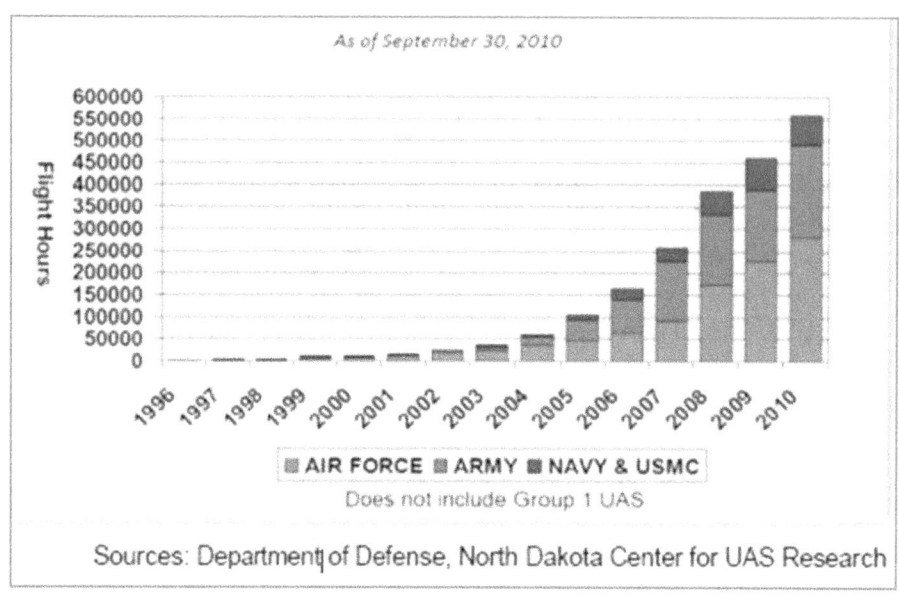

As of September 30, 2010

Flight Hours

■ AIR FORCE ■ ARMY ■ NAVY & USMC

Does not include Group 1 UAS

Sources: Department of Defense, North Dakota Center for UAS Research

Figure 1. Exponential Increase in RPA Flight Hours

(North Central Texas Regional General Aviation and Heliport System Plant, 2011)

Furthermore, in a 2011 USA Today article, Lt General Larry James reports that daily combat missions for operators of Predators and Reapers have quadrupled from 10 to 15 in 2007 to 57 today. According to James, "We've kind of been in this almost constant surge mode because there's such a demand for this capability, really for four to five years" (Zoroya, 2011).

Mets (2010) outlines the many advantages that RPAs have to offer. Most of the advantages stem from the removal of human limitations in the system: less required safety margin; saved weight, space and money through the removal of life support systems; enhanced maneuverability; extended loiter time ability; and reduced fuel costs. Taken together, these items all contribute to a reduction in the number of aircraft required. Further, the development time for these platforms have been shorter than in manned systems which truncates the acquisition cycle and increases the vehicles' useful service lives before becoming obsolete. Additionally, the Remote Split Operations

(RSO) concept reduces the effective footprint of military forces in the combat theater. In turn, this reduces the support structure required to sustain operations at deployed locations and enhances political goals in theater when excessive troop presence is detrimental. Additionally, "building a long-range RPA with stealthy, high speed, and air refueling capabilities might well overcome the limitations caused by the reductions in US forward force stationing" (Mets, 2010:20-21).

The list of advantages paints a pretty rosy picture; however, Mets (2010) does concede several shortfalls when it comes to RPAs. First, the RSO scheme described above is highly dependent on nearly instant, global communications; there are a myriad of ways to disrupt these systems. While individual RPAs themselves are relatively cheap, the associated equipment used to control them and the hardening of these systems against adversary countermeasures is not. To date, RPAs have typically operated in a fairly permissive airspace environment; RPAs would need to become more survivable to operate in areas with more formidable air defense systems. As alluded to earlier, culture poses a significant roadblock. The USAF culture still presents a challenge with respect to personnel problems in connection with RPA manning. Another issue is that of command and control; both manned aircraft and RPAs started out as ISR platforms, but the addition of lethal capabilities has generated contention for control by authorities even at the same level of command. Finally, some experts have foreshadowed ethical issues, in that RPAs will enable leaders to contemplate risk-free combat, allowing them to consider war more thinkable (rather than unthinkable) than it really should be (Mets, 2010).

During an address at Maxwell AFB in 2008, Secretary of Defense, Robert Gates remarked on the numerous cultural obstacles RPAs have faced throughout their evolution: "All of the services must examine their cultures critically if we are to have the capabilities relevant and necessary to overcome the most likely threats Americans will face in the years to come" (Gates, 2008) He offered RPAs as his case in point, asserting that unmanned systems cost less and offer greater loiter times than their manned counterparts, making them ideal for many of today's tasks. In the Secretary's view, more can and should be done to meet the needs of the men and women fighting in current conflicts. He called for a rethinking of longstanding service assumptions and priorities about which missions will require certified pilots and which do not; whether low-cost, low-tech alternatives exist to do basic reconnaissance and close air support…aircraft our partners can also afford (Gates, 2008).

This cultural impediment described by Gates has infected the procurement process as well. Stulberg (2007) asserted that the USAF has been chided repeatedly for rushed development and immature acquisitions marred by shifting requirements, configuration problems, spiraling costs and poor reliability. Furthermore, the USAF conceded sole direction for the Joint Unmanned Combat Air System (J-UCAS) program to the USN and remained noncommittal about future support for the development of a "common operating system" for multiple unmanned platforms or reliance on UAS for long-range strike missions (Stulberg, 2007). Yet, in 2004, a US Government Accountability Office report recommended that rather than have each armed service conduct separate research and development of UAS platforms that will not be interoperable, it would be more economical and efficient to look at desired capabilities and build a joint UAS platform. Again, this suggestion is reminiscent of Von Karman's

22

advice of nearly 60 years prior to establish centers for the development of a particular process or task, rather than attempt these creations in multiple isolated centers.

The operation of RPAs in the National Air Space (NAS) has proven a significant roadblock to their ultimate integration with manned flight. Barnhart, Hoffman, Marshall, and Shappee (2012) affirm that there exists no specific reference in the Federal Aviation Regulations (FARs) to unmanned aircraft, pilots and operators of unmanned aircraft, or the operation in the NAS of unmanned aircraft. In fact, if one is to adhere to the strict definition, an unmanned aircraft is an "aircraft" and there is no exception found elsewhere in the regulations that excludes RPAs from that definition, thus, in this interpretation, all rules that apply to manned aircraft would also apply to unmanned aircraft. Obviously, this poses several problems. For one, if RPA operators were strictly held to the "see and avoid" requirements, there would be no RPA flights in civil airspace! The Federal Aviation Administration (FAA) recognizes that a certifiable "detect, sense, and avoid" solution to the "see and avoid" problem for RPAs is still many years away. According to Barnhart, et al., (2012) there are currently only two ways to operate RPAs in the NAS: via a Certificate of Authorization (COA) available only to public entities or via an experimental airworthiness certificate.

As per Barnhart et al. (2012), there are two issues facing the FAA with respect to its enforcement authority. First, it must determine what it *can* regulate. Second, it must decide what it *will* regulate. These determinations depend greatly on the interpretation of what constitutes an "aircraft." While there have not yet been any formal legal challenges to the FAA's enforcement authority over unmanned aircraft and their operations, there is significant pressure for the FAA to take the lead in RPA rule making. Unfortunately, the

FAA enforcement toolbox may be lacking in substance when it comes to dealing with ignorant, uncooperative, or openly defiant RPA operators. In the words of Barnhart et al. (2012:47),

> As market forces create greater opportunities for developers and entrepreneurs to invest capital into more sophisticated systems and bring the industry closer to solving the sense-and-avoid problem, there will be ever increasing pressure on the FAA to put into place a regulatory structure that will allow the agency to reclaim its "ownership" of the airspace.

Lee (2011) highlights the issue of trust with respect to RPAs. In her view, RPAs today are far from inspiring the level of confidence necessary for their successful development and integration. She asserts that this trust must approach that of humans charged with executing missions and is built incrementally over time. She further points out that technology is not the limiting factor; instead, policy will ultimately stunt integration.

Another barrier is the cultural challenge. Fitzsimonds and Mahnken (2007) attest that transitions from one type of military approach or system to very different operational concepts or technologies have a major impact on the individuals within these societies. In concert with Max Planck's quote that opens Chapter 1, cultural change within the military is so difficult that any major peacetime innovation requires a full generation to complete; enough time for a new cadre of junior officers practicing the new technique to rise to positions of leadership. Yet, Fitzsimonds and Mahnken's (2007) research refutes the stereotypical notion of conservative senior officers squelching the innovative ferment within the junior ranks. In fact, the survey they conducted corroborates conclusions made by other experts, revealing no widespread or deep-seated opposition to RPAs beyond the technological uncertainty. The large-scale introduction of RPAs would, however, change the very ethos of flying. It would alter the traditional sense of authority and responsibility for assessing risk and applying lethal force. There would be diminished opportunities for battlefield valor; as one service member put it, "there wouldn't be enough danger to give us glory" (Fitzsimonds and Mahnken, 2007:100). Still, Fitzsimonds and Mahnken's (2007) survey found senior officers showed more receptivity to RPAs and the ensuing changes wrought by their incorporation than did junior officers. Additionally, senior officers were more open to the cultural change to the institution of flying (Fitzsimonds and Mahnken, 2007).

Marriage of Air Refueling and Remotely Piloted Aircraft

The "FY2009-2034 Unmanned Systems Integrated Roadmap" addresses unmanned aerial systems as they apply to the nine Joint Capability Areas (JCA). It names the AR of unmanned aerial systems in association with two of the nine JCAs: logistics and building partnerships. The roadmap further specifies that tanker unmanned RPA systems capable of automatically air-refueling USAF or sister Service and coalition aircraft with compatible AR systems will enter research, development, test and evaluation from 2020 to 2025, procurement from 2025 to 2029 and fielding in the USAF inventory from 2026 on (DoD, 2009).

On the international front, the JAPCC (2007) recognized several categories in the marriage of these two technologies: unmanned tankers and unmanned receivers. The organization argued that air forces and industry exploring the development of unmanned tankers is limited, so far, to very small tankers refueling other RPAs. Hence, this is the logical first step in the marriage because it minimizes the challenges of air-refueling the current light RPAs with a large tanker. Additionally, it avoids the challenge of operating manned and unmanned systems in close proximity. While at the time of the JAPCC article, there existed a significant dearth of research and development in the area of large unmanned tankers, the experimental refueling of RPAs was proceeding quite rapidly. Accordingly, two potential modes for RPA AR were identified: refueling current RPAs such as the Predator or Global Hawk, and air-refueling a future generation of RPAs similar to today's manned aircraft such as F-16 or F-35 drones. Consequently, the JAPCC (2007) argued that although there were currently no requirements for air-refuelable RPAs or for RPA AR, the future development of RPA AR could ultimately drive requirements for RPA tankers. Further, the JAPCC (2007) maintained that probe and drogue AR would be the most practical system for RPA tankers since it permits a more passive operation for tanker systems in contrast to boom AR. Finally, the JAPCC (2007) also posits that until RPA tankers become interoperable and separable from a specific receiver unit and location, the likely solution will be to keep the RPA tanker under the authority and operation of the supported receiver unit. This would be a significant departure from the current tanker command and control construct.

The marriage of AR capability with the technology of RPAs is mentioned in several official AF documents as well, to include the USAF "UAS Roadmap" and the "Air Mobility Master Plan" (AMMP). The "UAS Roadmap" identifies several platforms that will become AR capable. The MQ-M will evolve to include an AR configuration in the 2030 timeframe which will allow it to serve as a tanker. The MQ-Mb is slated to merge capabilities of several other platforms to create one system with a wider spectrum of capabilities, to include the ability to conduct receiver AR. The MQ-Lc, a common core airframe, will serve as the foundation for all missions requiring a large aircraft platform. It will harness autonomous and modular technologies to present many capabilities to the Joint Force Commander, to include AR. The document identifies automatic AR on the long term path towards full autonomy during the FY2015 to 2025 timeframe and names Air Mobility Command (AMC) as the lead Major Command (MAJCOM) for the AR of UAS (HQUSAF, 2009).

AMC addresses the combination of RPAs and AR in its future air mobility concepts section. AMC maintains that its overall goal is to meet global AR requirements; the command acknowledges, however, that those requirements are not expected to diminish in the coming years. In fact, AR requirements may increase over the next 25 years and beyond. The two main reasons for this upward trend are the increasing challenges of regional A2/AD strategies, as well as the development and fielding of unmanned combat air systems. Both developments will drive AR requirements above and beyond what we see today (AAMP, 2012). While these texts merely touch on the idea of merging AR and RPAs, several reputable studies have been conducted that drive home the importance of investing in the concept.

Conceptual Progress

Stephenson (1999) examined the development of AR methods for RPAs from the standpoint of a manned tanker air-refueling an unmanned platform. He posits, that even though the USAF had no refuelable RPAs at the time of the study, the best solution to the RPA endurance problem would be to make them air-refuelable. He argued that doing so could triple their loiter time, allowing a single RPA to perform the missions of up to three non-refuelable RPAs. The result would be a reduced footprint of American presence overseas, a decrease in maintenance and production costs, and large logistical cost savings. Further, RPAs that are currently limited by the weight of their onboard equipment could trade range for payload and significantly reduce lapses in coverage. He maintained that the bottom line would be boosted mission performance and duration while realizing tremendous savings in production, maintenance and modification programs.

Stephenson (1999) identified the RPA best suited for retrofit and design with an AR system, the most effective rendezvous type and the best method for controlling the aircraft during AR. Through an analysis of four key issues influencing the AR of RPAs to include survivability, operational radius and mission duration, range versus payload, and adverse weather, Stephenson (1999) named the Global Hawk as the most appropriate of the USAF's current inventory to explore for applications in AR. He also argued for the en-route rendezvous as the best rejoin method since it allows the tanker to meet the RPA closer to its theater of operations, enables the join up to occur sooner (which equates to passing the gas sooner), and finally reduces the maneuvering required by both the tanker and the RPA. He closed with a notable contention for utilizing a secondary boom operator aboard the tanker aircraft to control the RPA from one mile in trail throughout the AR. He made his case stating that this arrangement would reduce the impact of time delay between control inputs and RPA reaction, and would eliminate the reliance on satellite radios for communication between the receiver and the boom operator. He further argued that the combination of a video display along with actual visual confirmation for the secondary boom operator controlling the RPA would enhance the mission effectiveness rate since the secondary boom operator could visually hand-fly the craft should the video data link be lost (Stephenson, 1999). Ultimately, he acknowledged that the biggest obstacle to this marriage remains "our personal and institutional prejudices and bias" (Stephenson, 1999:41). He closed his study with the notable contention that clearly a refuelable RPA can perform an almost unlimited number and variety of missions, while also affording tremendous capabilities that a manned platform simply cannot provide.

General Ronald Fogelman stated "I think UAVs are moving in the right direction – that is, initially we'll use them for intelligence, surveillance, reconnaissance and hopefully for longer dwell, greater survivability kinds of things. In the longer term though, we'll have to look at whether a 'smart' UAV is really the way to deliver weapons" (Thompson, 2000:22). Hence, the USAF commenced researching other combat missions ideas for UAVs, coining the term Unmanned (or Uninhabited) Combat Air Vehicle (UCAV). Calls for rapid development of UCAVs came from three directions, to include the USAF Scientific Advisory Board's New World Vistas report, the Defense Advanced Research Projects Agency (DARPA) office and the Air Force 2025 Project. As such, Thompson (2000) argued for the modification of some F-16C fighter aircraft into dual-role UCAVs as a means to quickly provide a cost-effective, unmanned military option. He goes on to state that at that time, the US needed an interim UCAV option to overcome cruise missile limitations as soon as possible.

Thompson's (2000) arguments for the development of UCAVs at the time was a result of advancing technology, political support, and most importantly, smaller military budgets that would eventually persuade the USAF to operate unmanned lethal aircraft for most combat missions in the future. He avowed that UCAVs would save up to 55 to 80 percent in flight operations and support costs as compared to unmanned systems due to the following advantages: lower vehicle cost, greater range and endurance, no crew risk, survivability which equates to reusability, no dependence on weather or maintenance ready aircraft for training through the use of simulators, lower training and support costs and fewer personnel required.

Thompson (2000), who advocated for the development of the UCAV over a decade ago, identified AR as a future UCAV concern due to transoceanic deployment distances and communication, risk to KC-135 and KC-10 high value assets, and coordination of tanker join-up and multi-aircraft refueling. He recognized that the primary obstacle for an F-16 UCAV program would be its limited combat range without AR. He proposed one idea: to add a small camera near the heads-up display at a look-up angle so that the remote ground or tanker-based operator could fly off the AR position lights mounted on the bottom of the tanker. While he believed that unmanned AR was already feasible with the existing technology at the time of his report, he also acknowledged the risk inherent in air refueling an unmanned aircraft within a few feet of a high value tanker asset. Hence, even with the advanced technology, he noted that many years of testing and, more importantly, KC-135 and KC-10 manned tanker acceptance were needed prerequisites for UCAV remote control AR (Thompson, 2000).

Basom (2007) addressed the following research question in his study: during future operations, what will the role of AR and unmanned aircraft systems be, particularly through the year 2025? He compared the advantages and disadvantages of air-refuelable versus non-air-refuelable RPAs and considered limitations of RPA technology at that time. He utilized an Army Field Manual's tool for testing solutions that examines feasibility, acceptability, suitability and completeness as the framework for his research. Through an intensely thorough review of literature, as well as in-depth interviews with experts in the field, Basom (2007) concluded that the benefits gained from air-refuelable RPAs are great and give leadership more options for accomplishing dull, dirty and dangerous missions. He foreshadowed a time when technology would allow RPAs to stay airborne for longer periods without AR or maintenance checks, but, until then, the marriage of RPA assets and AR capability would only increase in frequency across the full spectrum of US governmental operations (Basom, 2007).

At the time of Mazzara's (2009) research, various studies had suggested the possible benefits of air-refueling RPAs; his research filled a knowledge gap by quantifying the costs and benefits of doing so. His study stemmed from the same mindset of Stephenson's study, in that it considered the AR of unmanned platforms using today's existing manned tanker fleet. Further, he extended Stephenson's assertion that the Global Hawk is the UAV best suited to retrofit as an air-refuelable platform by using it as the template platform to perform his cost-benefit analysis. Using a linear program, Mazzara (2009) determined an appropriate number of RQ-4s to provide coverage over an area roughly the size of Iraq, given a 15 minute response time. He assumed that this minimum number must remain airborne at all times to supply combatant commanders with persistent ISR coverage. Contrary to Stephenson's identification of the en-route rendezvous as the most appropriate for this mission, Mazzara (2009) considered an anchor area. His analysis offered a side-by-side comparison of a mission scenario without AR and a 34 hour duration, and a mission scenario with AR and a 168 hour duration. The longer duration mission was enabled through five AR events spread throughout the flight at 32 hour intervals. He examined benefits in terms of reduced safety mishaps, reduced maintenance and flight costs, and increased operational efficiency. The only cost he considered was that of tanker support; more information concerning acquisition costs as well as training required for tanker crews would inevitably change his results. His findings revealed a net savings of over $3 million per year, hence he concluded that there would indeed be a quantifiable cost savings through the use of the Global Hawk as an air-refuelable platform to increase its persistence (Mazzara, 2009).

Technological Progress

DARPA completed its Autonomous Airborne Refueling Demonstration (AARD) program in 2007, showing that unmanned aircraft can autonomously perform in-flight refueling under operational conditions with a current manned tanker platform (Figure 7).

Several control techniques were tested, and the best was 100 percent effective in 18 attempted probe-and-drogue connections, the most challenging of which were characterized by up to five feet of peak-to peak drogue motion, approaching the limits of manned AR operations. The test further demonstrated the ability to make contact during turns, which typically is not attempted in manned AR operations. Finally, the test also demonstrated the ability to join the tanker from up to two nautical miles behind, 1000 feet below and 30 degrees off heading, thus providing a ready transition from the waypoint control approach used by most unmanned aircraft to a fully autonomous refueling mode. Two major enhancements resulted in the successful demonstrations. First, improved video processing eliminated troublesome dropouts, allowing the system to conduct four times as many plug attempts per flight. Second, advanced control algorithms proved capable of anticipating much of the overall drogue motion, actually matching the drogue motion precisely (Interavia Business & Technology, 2007).

Mammarella, Campa, Napolitano and Fravolini (2008) affirm that one of the biggest current limitations to RPAs is their inability to AR. One of the key issues contributing to this inability is the need for accurate measurement of the "tanker-UAV" position and orientation from the "pre-contact" position to the "astern" position. They allege that using RPA GPS signals for this task may not always be possible since the signals may be distorted by the tanker airframe. They investigated the use of Machine Vision (MV) technology, which assumes the availability of a digital camera installed on the UAV to provide imagery of the target. They further assume that the tanker and RPA can share a short-range data communication link during the docking maneuver. They proposed two different algorithms to solve the "Point Matching" problem; from a control point of view, the objective is to guide the RPA within a defined 3-dimensional window or "refueling box" below the tanker where the boom operator can then achieve a contact (Mammarella et al., 2008).

Rosenberg (2010) highlighted an exciting development in the field of unmanned AR when Northrop Grumman received a $33 million contract from DARPA for the KQ-X. This program aligns with Stephenson and Mazzara's predictions in that it uses the Global Hawk as a receiver RPA. Its purpose is to demonstrate the AR of a NASA Global Hawk by a sister ship and involves the retrofitting of two RQ-4s so that one can pump fuel into the other in-flight through a hose-and-drogue refueling system. The program will demonstrate a number of firsts, to include the first AR of an existing RPA platform, the first autonomous AR operation and the first flight of high-altitude, long-endurance RPAs in formation. According to Carl Johnson, Vice President of Advanced Concepts at Northrop Grumman Aerospace Systems, "Demonstrating the refueling of one UAV by another is a historic milestone" (Rosenberg, 2010:2).

In a "risk reduction flight test" conducted in January of 2011, a NASA Global Hawk played the role of tanker while Northrop Grumman's Proteus test aircraft, a manned RPA surrogate, acted as the receiver aircraft in search of the boom. The interaction took place at 45,000 feet and brought the two aircraft as close as only 45 feet (Figure 8). According to Geoffrey Sommer, KQ-X program manager, "Demonstrating close formation flight of two high-altitude aircraft, whether manned or unmanned, is a notable accomplishment" (Skillings, 2011:2).

The January flight shown above was a prelude to an actual autonomous aerial refueling involving two Global Hawks, scheduled for the spring of 2012. A striking paradigm shift in Northrop Grumman's plan places the tanker aircraft behind the receiver aircraft, as displayed in Figure 9. In this reverse refueling arrangement, the tanker is equipped with a refueling probe, and the tanker rendezvous' with the receiver, maneuvers into contact with the drogue and basket assembly of the receiver, and pushes fuel forward. Ultimately, this arrangement reduces cost because fewer aircraft would require permanent modifications (Warwick, 2010).

Shaker (1988) writes that the tele-operators of our current RPA platforms are the most sophisticated type of remote controlled vehicles that rely on advanced sensor systems. There are, however, some downsides to this technology. If the communication relays between the operator and vehicle are jammed or disrupted, the vehicle loses its functionality. Operator controlled machines may actually perform certain activities much slower than a robot relying on artificial intelligence. Finally, the operator, or UAS control system, may become a highly prized target to render the vehicle useless. Another issue, as Lane (2007) points out, is the time delay between the operator and the vehicle. The MQ-1 Predator, for instance, suffers from a 1.5 to 3 second time delay, an impediment which could have devastating effects to both tanker and receiver during AR.

Cummings (2008:1) identified human supervisory control as "intermittent human operator interaction with a remote, automated system in order to manage a controlled process or task environment." Thus, she makes the distinction between humans-ON-the-loop and humans-in-the-loop. She further describes this interdisciplinary field as consisting of three main characteristics: the psychology of human decision making, computer science, and systems engineering. She concedes that even the most elegantly designed systems will perform at a subpar level unless human interactions are taken into account (Cummings, 2008).

This assertion is consistent with Maybury's (2011) findings of early systems such as the Predator that were rapidly developed as Advanced Concept Technology Demonstrations (ACTDs). According to an RPA study of the AF Scientific Advisory Board (SAB), "poorly-designed Operator Control Stations (OCS) fail to provide effective, robust, and safe mission management" (Zacharias and Maybury, 2010). Limitations of the ACTD process are solutions that do not fully address the full spectrum of requirements, such as reliability, affordability, security, or usability. Thus, poor physical ergonomics are exacerbated by an excessive need for input, limited task awareness, and a lack of graceful degradation. The paradoxical result is that in spite of visual information overload, operators actually suffer sensory deprivation.

Maybury states "nowhere is the need for automation and enhancements to human-machine interaction more apparent than in the emerging area of RPAs operating with manned aircraft in national airspace" (2011). He asserts that overcoming current usability limitations can be accomplished through well designed cockpits and ground stations that consider human systems integration from the start. These developments will not only enhance human effectiveness, but also ensure more robust performance in the dull, dirty, or dangerous environments in which they are needed. He further posits that aside from the increased resiliency and performance that autonomy can provide, it also adds benefits such as efficiency, speed, and predictability if given well specified environmental conditions. Automation is valued both by society and the defense community; increasingly, escalating manpower requirements along with its associated costs are driving interest in autonomy because of its self-directed and self-sufficient characteristics (Maybury, 2011).

Lee (2011) concedes that currently there is no universally agreed upon definition of autonomy. A good starting point emerging within the scientific community, however, views the issue as degrees of RPA independence from human control. She cites Maybury's description of four levels of human control on the context of RPA design shown below in Table 2.

Table 2. Maybury's Levels of Human Control

Level	Description
1	"No Autonomy" = Full Manual Control
2	"Partial Automation" = Humans-IN-the-Loop
3	"Supervisory Control" = Humans-ON-the-Loop
4	Full Autonomy

Another widely accepted starting point for describing autonomy in terms of human control is shown in Figure 10. This is known by the scientific community as Sheridan and Verplank's levels of automation. This conceptualization views autonomy as a continuum, thus allowing RPA designers and operators to develop and employ decision aids for these aircraft at varying levels of autonomy on a case-by-case basis, depending on the RPAs mission (Lee, 2011).

While the above model acknowledges that autonomy entails more than an all-or-nothing view, it does not fully flesh out two other significant dimensions of autonomy: mission complexity and environmental complexity. Mission complexity measures an autonomous system's ability to perfume various mission and tasks. Environmental complexity, on the other hand, measures an autonomous system's ability to adapt and respond to changes in the environment. Figure 11 illustrates this multi-faceted view of autonomy which lends itself well to describing RPA operations in complex air environments (Lee, 2011). RPAs performing the AR mission would be operating in just such environments, thus, this model is important for future senior military officials to understand and internalize.

Competition

According to the DoD UAS Roadmap, many future propulsion and power systems are being examined for use in future unmanned aircraft. Fuel cell technology is expected to be the best compromise between efficiency and performance, as demonstrated by the many automotive companies who are experimenting with fuel cell technology implementation in cars (Basom, 2007). The Office of the SECDEF's view reinforces this point, stating that other technologies such as improved fuel cells contend with automated air refueling as a means for extending UAS missions.

Potential competitors with RPA AR are not that far off in the future. Boeing is working on Phantom Eye, an RPA fueled by hydrogen and intended to fly at 65,000 feet for four days. In January of 2011, Aerovironment's Global Observer made the first ever hydrogen powered RPA flight for just a few hours at low altitude, but this project's aim is to fly for a week at 65,000 feet. Solar power is also getting attention from the RPA industry. The company Qinetiq created Zephyr, an RPA which stayed aloft for 14 days nonstop in July of 2011. Additionally, Boeing has produced Solar Eagle, whose short term goal is to stay aloft for 30 days but whose more ambitious long-term goal is to remain aloft for five years (Skillings, 2011).

Barnhart et al. (2012) list several other power solutions that may have an impact on the relative viability of RPA AR. In addition to the hydrogen and solar power mentioned above, bio-fuels may also prove as a viable, long-lasting energy source. Electric options may result in advancements that enable RPAs with the ability to replenish from power lines, an electric fuel "tanker" concept, or the transmission of electricity through the air from antennas to recharge onboard batteries. Finally, developments in structural materials will focus in large part on composite technology that will become lighter and more durable, as well as easier to manufacture, maintain and repair. Hence, in keeping with axiomatic nature of aircraft design, lighter weight equates to more payload carrying capacity.

The Future

Future applications of the marriage of RPAs with AR and the issues of interoperability are sure to extend not only to the US military, but also to other government agencies as well. Basom (2007) points to a future example in which a USAF tanker launches to air-refuel an RPA belonging to the Federal Emergency Management Agency (FEMA) performing as a communication platform or conducting damage assessment following a natural disaster; or that same tanker may air-refuel an RPA performing an ISR mission along the national border for the US Customs and Border Control Agency. The possibilities are endless. Persistent ISR tracking will remain the bedrock of military RPA missions, due to the high demand for information. As Donald Kerr, Director of the National Reconnaissance Office stated "The United States nearly got to Abu Musab al-Zarqawi, the leader of al-Qaida in Iraq, in 2003. Zarqawi, who was being tracked as a moving target at the time, got away because of a 20-second gap in coverage. In those 20 seconds, the trail went cold" (Schanz, 2006:20). Frustrating events such as this only serve to add fuel to the fire in the argument for proliferation of the RPA-AR combo to address limited range and limited access issues of current RPAs.

Identify the Capability Gap

A significant application for RPAs performing the AR mission is the ASBC approved by SECAF and SECNAV in the summer of 2011. The 2010 Quadrennial

Defense Review (QDR) actually directed development of the ASBC as part of its

guidance to rebalance the force:

> [Defeat] adversaries across the range of military operations, including adversaries equipped with sophisticated anti-access and area denial [A2/AD] capabilities. The concept will address how air and naval forces will integrate capabilities across all operational domains – air, sea, land, space, and cyberspace – to counter growing challenges to US freedom of action (DoD, 2010:32).

Carreno, Culora, Galdorisi and Hone (2010) attested that the idea of the ASBC

was driven by several converging trends. First was the Obama administration's decision

to draw down in Iraq and Afghanistan over a finite timeline, and shift emphasis away

from the war on terrorism. Second, was the startling rise of China over the past decade in

such a way that Admiral Robert Willard, Commander of the Pacific Theater noted,

"Elements of China's military modernization appears designed to challenge our freedom

of action in the region" (Carreno et al., 2010:6). Finally, a third issue was the

unanticipated economic recession faced by the US. Harrison (2010) maintains the

bottom line is that the fiscal reality in a flat or declining budgetary environment means

that the DoD cannot afford to continue funding both personnel accounts as well as

acquisitions accounts to the same extent that it does today (Carreno et al., 2010).

Two studies by the Center for Strategic and Budgetary Assessments highlight Iran

and China as catalysts behind the focus on the ASBC. Both nations appear to be

investing in capabilities to "raise precipitously over time – and perhaps prohibitively –

the cost to the US of projecting power into two areas of vital interest: the western Pacific

and the Persian Gulf" (Krepinevich, 2010:7). Carreno et al., (2010) acknowledge that the

US military may not have the strategic assets needed to deter and prevail against high-end peers such as China. They further argue that without better coordination between US military services, particularly the USN and the USAF, this outcome is all but guaranteed; joint air and naval planners must also go one step further to actually tie operational requirements to specific capabilities. While the ASBC is not specifically aimed at any particular country or region, the ultimate goal is to determine how combined USAF and USN capabilities can address these threats. In this sense, the concept must be viewed as more than simply doing more with less; instead, it is a return to historical precedents when compelling strategic and operational realities forced US naval and air forces to work together in a truly integrated fashion to project power against a determined foe. The purpose of the ASBC is to set the conditions for a favorable military balance in the Western Pacific. By creating a credible means to defeat A2/AD capabilities, the US can enhance stability in the region, ultimately lowering the possibility of escalation through deterrence. According to Van Tol (2010:95), "The most important question proponents of the ASBC must answer is whether the concept would help to restore and sustain a stable military balance in the Western Pacific." As Admiral Mike Mullen, chairman of the Joint Chiefs of Staff purports, the ASBC "is a prime example of how we need to keep breaking down stovepipes between services, between federal agencies, and even between nations" (Miles, 2010).

The ASBC strategy calls for mutual support between USN and USAF assets in which securing the Navy's freedom of maneuver precedes gaining forward operation of AF tankers and other support aircraft. ASBC fundamentals include, among others, *omnipresent unmanned* combat air systems to provide *persistent* ISR; increased, sustainable and survivable AR capacity; and a significant increase in long-range ISR assets like Global Hawk *with increased range* and sensors (Carreno et al., 2010). (Emphasis added by the researcher.)

AMC asserts that one concept to mitigate A2/AD is to employ unmanned combat air vehicles such as the Northrop Grumman X-47 or Boeing's Phantom Ray, both currently undergoing proof of concept testing. The command attests that in order to extend the combat range of these vehicles, they will need the capability to conduct AAR. Due to the increased potential of US military forces facing the A2/AD threat, AMC Future Concepts branch is beginning to explore the need for an advanced/unmanned tanker that would combine the capabilities of range, speed, low observable technology, advanced avionics, defensive systems and of course, AAR. The low observable characteristics of the KC-Z would fill a deficiency gap in survivability, absent in today's tanker aircraft, which are modified from large radar cross section commercial aircraft (HQ AMC/A8XPL, 2011).

A 2008 Bullet Background Paper from AMC/A8XC identified AAR as number eight on AMC's 2011 prioritized list of capability gaps. The paper acknowledged that with the proliferation of RPAs, there will be a need for AAR in the future, but a lack of current requirements had stifled continued development. It identified the Navy's Unmanned Carrier Launched Airborne Surveillance and Strike (N-UCLASS) system as possibly having an AR requirement. The paper calls for the Navy to define USAF requirements to air-refuel its N-UCLASS so that the USAF can reengage its AAR efforts which had recently lost funding to the Next Generation Long Range Strike Program (Middleton, n.d.).

Ewing (2011) reported that Boeing has received a $480,000 study contract from the USN; the eight month contract will conceptually demonstrate that an N-UCLASS system can provide persistent CVN-based ISR and strike capability supporting carrier air wing operations by 2018 when the Navy wants it in the fleet. RPA advocates assert that in tomorrow's conflicts, ships will need to keep ever-farther away from their targets due to A2/AD environments. Hence, only RPAs will have the stealth, range, ability to loiter and other advantages that the Navy needs. In essence, force extended RPAs are the key to the future relevance of aircraft carriers (Ewing, 2011).

Keller (2011) reports that aside from providing an unmanned aircraft capable of persistent surveillance and precision strike, the N-UCLASS will also be interoperable for joint forces at levels one to four per STANAG 4586. Austin (2010) explains that NATO aims to agree on common standards within the nation members for the design and operation of RPAs. The organization issues "Standardization Agreements" (STANAG) which are published in English and French. NATO recognized the need to ensure interoperability between its forces and produced NATO STANAG 4586 "UAS Control System Architecture" to achieve this. STANAG 4586 defines five levels of interoperability between RPAs of different origins with respect to the system's command and control interface, control stations, and data-link interface. These interoperability levels vary from 100% interoperability whereby one nation's control station can fully control another's RPA.

Pacific Command (PACOM) isn't the only theater that faces the challenge of a tyranny of distance. The Africa Command (AFRICOM) area of responsibility (AOR) currently confronts the same access issues foreshadowed by the ASBC. In comments made to the Advanced Study of Air Mobility class of 2012, Major General Woodward conceded that every commander wants more ISR (2012). Yet, the limited range of RPAs along with the delicate role that politics plays in their potential bed-down locations significantly hinders their usefulness on a continent the size of the USA, Europe, China and India put together (Figure 12).

5 Apr 12

Singer (2009) professed that beyond the major question of what happens when the robots of science fiction become political reality over the next few decades is the emerging concern that force planners must begin thinking about doctrine. He viewed the issue not as buying systems and arguing over who has control over them, but the much broader question of where and how it all fits together. Industry leaders criticize the military's practice of purchasing systems despite not fully developing operational plans for them. iRobot executives complain that the military is actually falling behind the technology in how it conceptualizes its use in the field, especially with respect to ignoring robots' growing smarts and autonomy. This point is underscored by the lack of an overall plan for support structures. Singer (2009) concluded that developing the right doctrine for using unmanned systems is essential to the future of the force.

III. Methodology

"Fatalism, in other words, has become a fatality."
- *Olaf Helmer*

A particular type of qualitative study, a grounded theory method, specifically, a Delphi study was used to tackle this problem. According to Lauer and Asher (1988), all inquiry starts out in qualitative form. As evidenced through the literature review, little consensus exists on this topic, the variables are unknown, and relevant theory is missing. Hence, a qualitative study is appropriate to define what is important; or, what needs to be studied (Leedy and Ormord, 2010). As Leedy and Ormord (2010) state, the main purpose of a grounded theory study is to begin with the data and use it to develop a theory. The grounded theory process uses a constant comparative method in which the researcher alternates between data collection and data analysis, with data analysis refining later data collection. The resulting theory that ultimately evolves includes numerous concepts and the interrelationships between those concepts; in other words, it has conceptual density (Leedy and Ormrod, 2010).

The Delphi Study

According to Cuhls (n.d.), the Delphi method was originally developed in the 1950s by the RAND (Research and Development) Corporation, however, its roots date as far back as 600 B.C. in ancient Greece. The foundation of the temple at Delphi and its oracle took place before recorded history. The temple was a locus of knowledge, the information coming in through the queries of ambassadors and recorded on either metal or stone plates. Thus, the Delphi monastery was one of the very few places on Earth where knowledge was accumulated, ordered and preserved. In essence, the Delphi oracle

49

was the largest database of the ancient world. The name "Delphi" was originally coined by Kaplan, an associate professor of philosophy working for the RAND Corporation on a project aimed at improving the use of expert predictions in policy making. He referred to the principle of the oracle as a non-falsifying prediction, in other words, a statement that does not have the property of being true or false. Hence, using the "Delphi" for the modern foresight method was more than just a brand name (Cuhls, n.d.). The following genealogical tree outlines the evolution of the Delphi method worldwide since its birth in ancient Greece (Figure 13) (The researcher acknowledges the misspelling of the word future as "FUTUR" in 1999).

Skulmoski, Hartman and Krahn (2007) attest that the first Delphi was developed by Norman Dalkey of the RAND Corporation in the 1950s for a US military sponsored project. Dalkey alleged that the goal of the project was "to solicit expert opinion to the selection, from the point of view of a Soviet strategic planner, of an optimal US industrial target system and to estimate the number of A-bombs required to reduce the munitions output by a prescribed amount" (Dalkey and Helmer, 1963:458). Linstone and Turoff (2002) state, the original "Project Delphi" was viewed as a spin-off of defense research whose purpose was to obtain the most reliable consensus of opinion from a group of experts via a series of intensive questionnaires interspersed with controlled opinion feedback. Rowe and Wright (1999) characterize a classic Delphi as having the following four key features: anonymity of Delphi participants, iteration, controlled feedback and statistical aggregation of group responses. The most important product of a Delphi is the reality defined through its interaction (Linstone and Turoff, 2002).

The Delphi method is an iterative process to collect and distill the anonymous judgments of experts using a series of data collection and analysis techniques interspersed with feedback (Skulmoski et.al., 2007). In essence, it is an cyclical approach that starts with vague, widely dispersed ideas and concepts. Through anonymous feedback facilitated by the researcher, the participants hone and focus their subsequent inputs, thus ultimately converging on the final answer. Skulmoski et al., (2007) assert that the Delphi method is well suited as a research instrument when there is incomplete knowledge about a problem or phenomena; it works especially well when the goal is to improve our understanding of problems, opportunities, solutions, or to develop forecasts.

A plethora of research supports their assertion, as illustrated by the data contained in this paragraph. Linstone and Turoff (2002) avow that a Delphi may be characterized as a method for structuring a group communication process so that the process is effective in allowing a group of individuals as a whole to deal with a complex problem. They affirm that the methodology focuses collective human intelligence on a problem at hand. Rowe and Wright (1999) state that the method can also be used as a judgment, decision-aiding or forecasting tool. Delbeq, Van de Ven and Gustafson (1975) extend this point stating that it can also be applied to program planning and administration. Adler and Ziglio (1996) support Delbeq's et al. (1975) assertion that the Delphi method can be used when there is incomplete knowledge about a problem or phenomena. They go on to say that the method can be applied to problems that do not lend themselves to precise analytical techniques. Additionally, Czinkota and Ronkainen (1997); Skulmoski, et al. (2007); and Skulmoski and Hartman (2002) corroborate the assertion that a Delphi is used to investigate that which does not yet exist. Rowe and Wright (1999) validate Cuhls' (n.d.) view that the Delphi method makes for better use of group interaction because nobody loses face since the survey is accomplished anonymously. Cuhls (n.d.) also points out that the Delphi method is especially useful for long-range forecasting of 20 to 30 years as expert opinions are the only source of information available. Further, Cuhls (n.d.) asserts that the Delphi method is based on structural surveys and makes use of the available intuitive information of the expert participants. It therefore delivers qualitative as well as quantitative results with underlying explorative, predictive and normative research elements. Cuhls (n.d.) further states that the Delphi method is mainly used when long-term issues have to be assessed. Eto (2003) asserts that the method is also suitable if there is the sometimes political attempt to involve many persons in a process.

Figure 14 displays a typical three round Delphi process. In deriving the research question, a literature review is conducted to determine if a theoretical gap exists. The Delphi method is chosen for research design when the researcher wants to collect the judgments of experts in a group decision making setting; both qualitative and quantitative methods can be used (Skulmoski et al., 2007). According to Adler and Ziglio (1996), there are four requirements for expertise that must be considered when selecting the research sample: knowledge and expertise with the issues under investigation; capacity and willingness to participate; sufficient time to participate; and effective communications skills. Cuhls (n.d.) recommends that a mixture of experts from industry, business, academia and research, as well as a demographically diverse sample mix should be invited to participate.

Schmidt (1997) maintains that in developing the first round questionnaire, the purpose sometimes is simply to brainstorm. A Delphi pilot study ought to be conducted with the goal of testing and adjusting the questionnaire to improve comprehension; this is especially important for inexperienced researchers to refine scope and time commitment. Once Round One results are analyzed according to the research paradigm, they form the basis for the Round Two questionnaire. Schmidt (1997) contends that Round Two should allow participants to verify their Round One responses, provide any feedback to other participants' responses, and finally, rank and rate the output of Round One. Again, Round Two responses are used to develop Round Three with additional questions to verify results, understand the boundaries of the research, as well as where the results can be extended. Ultimately, the Delphi results are verified, generalized and documented (Schmidt, 1997).

Skulmoski et al. (2007) highlight several methodological design decisions that must be addressed. First, initial questions are typically broad and open-ended so as to widely cast the research net. The result, however, is that more data is likely to be collected requiring more time consuming analysis. Second, true experts in a field have great insights, but typically are extremely strapped for time. Thus, engaging, concise, and well-written questions can often entice their participation. Third, there is quite a wide range of sample sizes in Delphi studies throughout history. There is a reduction in group error and a corresponding increase in decision quality as sample size increases. Also, the larger the group, the more convincingly the results can be said to be verified. Large, heterogeneous groups, however, greatly increase the complexity and difficulty of collecting data, reaching consensus, conducting analysis, and verifying the results. A further note is that potential sample size is positively related to the number of experts. Fourth, the number of rounds varies and depends on the purpose of the research; Delbeq et al. (1975) suggest that two to three iterations is sufficient for most research. Finally, the mode of interaction significantly affects the turn-around times between rounds and attrition. Electronic mail affords advantages to both researcher and participant. Its expediency helps keep enthusiasm alive and participation high (Skulmoski et al., 2007).

Likert Scale

The Likert response format is a method of attitude, opinion, or perception assessment of a uni-dimensional variable. The term was coined in recognition of Rensus Likert's contributions via his classic paper, "A Technique for the Measurement of Attitudes" in 1932 (Barnette, 2010). According to Riconscente and Romeo (2010), Likert tackled the issue facing social science researchers who wanted to quantitatively describe people's attitude or beliefs about an issue. Attitudes and beliefs, however, are qualitative and cannot be directly measured. Until the time of Likert's research, the best procedures available for measuring attitudes were those developed by Louis Thurstone. Likert identified two shortcoming of Thurstone's approach. First, it required many judges in a long and laborious process. Second, the use of his attitude scales made several statistical assumptions that had not yet been verified (Riconscente and Romeo, 2010). Thus, Likert set out to use some of the features of a Thurstone scale, but to simplify the process in the hopes of achieving a similar level of reliability (Barnette, 2010). The result was a more streamlined approach which is now the most widely used survey methodology in social science research and evaluation (Riconscente and Romeo, 2010).

According to Barnette (2010), the Likert scale provides a score based on a series of items that have two parts. One part is the stem that is a statement of fact or opinion to which the respondent is asked to react. The second part is the response scale itself. Riconscente and Romeo (2010) state that in Likert's study, each statement became a scale in and of itself, and a person's response to each statement was assigned a score. The response scores were then combined by using a median or a mean to obtain an attitude score. He found that many items had distributions resembling a normal distribution, thus he concluded that it was legitimate to determine a single uni-dimensional scale value finding the mean or sum of the items and using that for a value that represented the attitude of the variable on a continuum (Barnette, 2010).

Barnette (2010) identifies several types of response bias inherent in using the Likert scale. First, acquiescence bias is the tendency for the respondent to provide positive responses to all or almost all of the items. A long recommended practice for combating acquiescence bias is the use of negatively worded or reverse-worded Likert stems (Barnette, 2010). A drawback to this method is that the added cognitive complexity associated with negatively stated items results in lower levels of validity and reliability (Riconscente and Romeo, 2010).

Central tendency bias is the tendency to respond to all or most of the items with the middle response category. This particular bias can be addressed through the choice of either an odd or even number of response options and the clear labeling of the middle response. Most survey researchers feel that three categories is too few and more than seven is too many. Additionally, some assert that using an even number of responses forces those surveyed to choose one directional opinion or the other, while an odd number of responses allows for a neutral opinion (Barnette, 2010).

Finally, social desirability bias is the tendency for respondents to reply to items to reflect what they believe would be the expected response based on societal norms or values, rather than their own feelings. This situation is exacerbated if respondents have any feeling that their responses could be directly or even indirectly attributed to them personally (Barnette, 2010). This particular bias is inherently contested by the design of the Delphi method itself. Members of the expert panel in a Delphi are not to discuss their responses with other panel members.

Median and Inter-Quartile Range

According to Keeney, Hasson, and McKenna (2006:209-210), the primary purpose for using a Delphi process is to "gain consensus or judgment among a group of perceived experts on a topic." As such, the data collected in the second and third rounds is analyzed to determine if consensus has been reached. The criterion for measuring consensus and the level of consensus, however, is a bit of moving target and may vary from study to study (Raynes and Hahn, 2000). The data collected in the second round is analyzed to calculate the median and inter-quartile range (Jenkins and Smith, 1994) to identify items for which consensus was reached on their relative importance. Barnette (2010) affirms that the level of measurement in a Likert study is ordinal; comparisons then, ought to be measured via nonparametric methods. As such, the median or mean should be used when comparing scale indicators of central tendency.

A commonly used method for determining consensus is through the analysis of the inter-quartile range of the ratings (Raynes and Hahn, 2000; Rojewski and Meers,

1991). Raynes and Hahn (2000:311) state "the interquartile range is the absolute value of the differences between the 75th and the 25th percentiles, with smaller values indicating higher consensus." Further, an Inter-Quartile Range (IQR) that is 20% of the rating scale appears to be a conservative but acceptable criterion for determining consensus.

Farrell's Study

The Delphi method is applicable and appropriate for this study because, as Linstone and Turoff (2002) state, there exists a recognized need to structure a group communication process to obtain a useful result for the research objective. The intent is for the Delphi study to overcome the hierarchical and stovepiped nature of today's military, ultimately even transcending the barriers between sister services and even the public and private sector. Farrell's (2010) study titled "Remotely Piloted Aircraft (RPA) Performing the Airdrop Mission" used a four round Policy Delphi study to determine the potential utility, benefits, drawbacks and pitfalls of utilizing RPA to perform the airdrop mission.

According to Farrell (2011:17-18), the research questions attempted to "encapsulate the questions that would be raised during the initial policy discussions at the general officer level in order to reduce the length of a future staffing process and improve the quality of responses by drawing on a diverse panel of experts while removing interpersonal dynamics." Farrell's Delphi research questions are shown below in Table 3:

Table 3: RPAs Performing the Airdrop Mission Delphi Research Questions

1) What are the airdrop roles and mission types that the MQ-9 Reaper could be utilized in without major structural changes to the aircraft?
2) What are the advantages to be gained over current airdrop platforms, including new mission sets that could be created, by utilizing the MQ-9 Reaper for airdrop?
3) What are the unavoidable drawbacks of utilizing the MQ-9 Reaper for airdrop?
4) What are the difficulties that need to be addressed early in prototyping, planning, procurement, or training in order to successfully utilize the MQ-9 Reaper for airdrop?

Farrell's (2011) study illuminated a number of possible uses of the MQ-9 for airdrop with the most useful being the ability to acquire imagery and point of impact coordinate updates in a dynamic environment. Further, the panel believed there would be distinct advantages to be gained by MQ-9 airdrop over current manned airdrop platforms, the most important being mitigating risk to manned aircraft in elevated threat environments. The unavoidable drawbacks that the panel named included a relatively limited payload capacity and the competition of airdrop with other missions of the MQ-9. Finally, Farrell's panel was able to distinguish several difficulties that need to be addressed in order to successfully utilize the MQ-9 for the airdrop mission. His overall impression of his panel's opinion was that the MQ-9 RPA capabilities should be developed to support both manned airdrop for large resupply missions as well as to conduct small, especially persistent resupply missions autonomously (Farrell, 2011).

One of the acknowledged limitations of Farrell's (2011) study was the lack of participation from General Officer, Flag Officer, or Senior Executive Service (SES) personnel. He asserted that while the expert panel was certainly robust, the study lacked perspective from senior decision makers that was critically desired (Farrell, 2011).

RPAs Performing the AR Mission Delphi Process

This study was planned as a three round Delphi; Farrell's study provided an excellent template for this study. The first round consisted of the five open-ended questions shown in Table 1. The line of questioning in this study and the order in which they were administered mirrored Farrell's research questions. Questionnaires for each round underwent peer review by my classmates in the Advanced Study of Air Mobility. All processing of surveys was conducted electronically.

As the Delphi facilitator, I developed the Round Two questionnaire based on the participant response from Round One. Since the Likert stems in a Delphi study are generated directly from the panel responses in Round One, I accepted the risk of acquiescence bias and minimized the editing of statements provided by the experts. In turn, this preserved the original intent of participant responses. The study utilized the following 5-point Likert scale (Table 4) derived from the "Likert Scale" (n.d.) as the most popular scale for agreement:

Table 4. Likert Scale

Rating	Meaning
5	Strongly Agree
4	Agree
3	Undecided
2	Disagree
1	Strongly Disagree

This scale addresses central tendency bias in that it uses the recommended five rating possibilities which allows allows for a neutral opinion.

To combat social desirability bias, the panel members in this particular study were not told who the other panel members were, and were directed not to speak with other panel members during the course of the study. Further, statements of confidentiality, voluntary consent, and adverse impact were reiterated to respondents during every round of the study. Additionally, the research underwent approval by the Air Force Institution of Technology (AFIT) Institutional Review Board (IRB) to enhance its legitimacy and credibility.

In keeping with the studies outlined above, I chose the median as the statistical measure, along with the IQR to define consensus. Using the 5-point Likert Scale for this study, 20% of five equates to achieving consensus at an IQR of one or below.

The Third Round consisted of providing the statistical information described above, as well as any comments made by panel members. The experts were then given the opportunity to rerate based on the group's initial consensus.

The concept of using RPAs as tankers to air-refuel other RPAs relates to a wide breadth of stakeholders. These include operators and experts both in AMC and Air Combat Command (ACC), scientists at the Headquarter Air Force (HAF) level, experts in the Automated Air-Refueling division at the Air Force Research Laboratory (AFRL), Project Air Force (PAF) through RAND Corporation, NASA, the FAA, civilian partner companies who already have or are developing this capability such as the Sierra Nevada Corporation, sister service experts working to develop systems such as the N-UCLASS, and of course, senior military leaders, just to name a few. Coordination for participation of potential expert panel members was accomplished with guidance from the sponsors of the research. Ultimately, five experts participated in the study.

Acknowledging the importance of the senior military leader perspective, as well as the shortcomings of Farrell's research without that viewpoint, I wanted to obtain SL participation in such a way that would minimize their time requirements. Thus, in coordination with the sponsors, I deviated from the traditional Delphi process by adding a separate, single round that targeted this particular demographic. The Senior Leader Round mirrored that of Round Two for the expert panel, and was sent electronically on behalf of the researcher by sponsor, Maj Gen Woodward. Ultimately, six senior military leaders responded.

Assumptions & Limitations

There are several assumptions and limitations inherent in this research. First, only unclassified sources are used. While a Delphi study generally has little internal validity, it inherently uses triangulation to obtain multiple sources of data with the hope of finding convergence. Likewise, I resisted the low external validity inherent in the Delphi study by choosing a representative sample for the panel of experts and SL to survey. Additional strategies for enhancing the credibility of the study include a thick description, feedback from colleagues and respondent validation. Researcher bias is always a potential limitation and was challenged through obtaining peer reviews and multiple scholarly opinions throughout the process.

According to Cuhls (n.d.), the Delphi can only provide potential answers to those problems which are identifiable today. Further, the entire procedure must be fixed in advance, so the logistics must be organized. Delphi surveys tend to belong to the more research-intensive foresight approaches. Moreover, potential bias exists in that expert assessments are not always objective (Cuhls, n.d.). The concept of using RPAs as air-refuelers requires a far-reaching breadth of coordination between stakeholders. Communication between these various players is critical to solving the issue at hand;

unfortunately, only five experts and six senior military leaders ultimately participated, corresponding to a relatively reduced decision quality of the results.

Riconscente and Romeo (2010) acknowledge several shortcomings of Likert scaling, despite its many advantages. First, Likert's method assumes that participants' responses refer wholly to the properties of the attitude or the latent trait being measured. In reality, respondents might agree or disagree with a statement for any number of reasons aside from the attitude of interest. Another major issue with Likert scaling is that it tends to confound two dimensions of an attitude: direction and intensity. Hence, the scales do not necessarily yield uni-dimensional ordinal scores (Riconscente and Romeo, 2010).

IV. Results and Analysis

"It requires a very unusual mind to undertake the analysis of the obvious."
-   Alfred North Whitehead

Expert Panel Composition

The expert panel consisted of the following five members in Table 5:

Table 5. Expert Panel Members

NAVAIR Acquisitions / systems engineer with 19 years total experience & 2 years specifically in RPA AR
AMC Senior Analyst / 30 years experience in air-refueling & 3 years in RPAs
RPA Evaluator & Weapons Instructor Course (WIC) Pilot / 4 years experience with AR in F-16 & 7+ years in RPAs
Sierra Nevada Corporation Navigation Engineer / 37 years total experience with12 years in RPA landing guidance & 3 years specifically in RPA AR
RPA Evaluator & Operational Test Pilot / 4 years experience with AR in KC-10 & 4.5 years in RPAs

Of note, the panel included three members of the USAF, to include AMC and ACC, as well as a potential "customer" in the USN engineer, and an engineer from private industry.

Round One

In addition to several background questions to assess the composition of the panel itself, the Round One questionnaire consisted of one basic rating question and five open-ended questions intended to draw out ideas from the experts. Thus, as the researcher, I facilitated a non-attribution brain storming session free from groupthink. The Round One questionnaire can be found in Appendix A.

The panel was first asked to rate the following statement: "RPAs could serve as tankers to perform the AR mission against receiver RPAs" using the Likert scale described in Chapter 3. The arithmetic median of the responses was 5 with an IQR of 0 indicating that the expert panel overwhelmingly agreed with the statement.

The responses to the five open-ended questions ranged from one-line sentences to multiple paragraphs. From these response, the researcher was able to distinguish 3 ideas for question one, 6 ideas for question two, 15 ideas for question three, 6 ideas for question four and 13 ideas for question five. These ideas formed the rating criterion used in Round Two.

Incidentally, expert panel responses to questions one and three included the answer "None." Including this possible answer in the Round Two rating exercise was consistent with Barnette's (2010) recommended tactic of using a negatively worded Likert stem to combat acquiescence bias. Also consistent with Barnette's (2010) assertions was the drawback that this method adds cognitive complexity. This was illustrated by several of the respondents leaving this rating stem blank in Round Two and having to be prompted for their answer.

Round Two

The Round Two Questionnaire can be found in Appendix B. In Round Two, the respondents were asked to use a Likert rating system to evaluate each of the ideas gleaned from the Round One open responses. The researcher then assessed each of the responses using the arithmetic median and IQR to determine consensus. Using this method, the expert panel found preliminary consensus on the following ideas in Table 6:

Table 6. Round Two Consensus Items

Question & Criteria	Rating
2) What advantages are to be gained over manned air-refueling platforms, including new mission sets that could be created, by utilizing RPAs as tankers to air-refuel receiver RPAs?	
Longer loiter times	Strongly Agree
Availability of enhanced aerodynamics and stealthier shapes	Agree
Reduced AR on-load times due to more reliable rejoins, contacts, and station keeping	Agree
More efficient use of low density, high demand assets	Agree
3) What are the unavoidable drawbacks are of utilizing RPAs to air refuel receiver RPAs?	
Need to prevent enemy interference (anti-tamper, anti-spoofing) with the vehicle	Strongly Agree
Technology development	Agree
Link robustness	Agree
Lost link protocols	Agree
Contingency management	Agree
Lack of understanding in proper employment of RPAs	Agree
Aviator perception of RPAs	Undecided
Need for an airpower practitioner to influence RPA tasking system	Undecided
Reliability, consistency, and operational readiness	Undecided
Bed-down and maintenance	Undecided
High cost	Undecided
4) What difficulties need to be addressed early in prototyping, planning, procurement, or training in order to successfully utilize RPAs as tankers to air-refuel receiver RPAs?	
Hand-off between beyond line of sight to line of sight data link systems	Undecided
Develop prognostic health and service life surveillance to enable on-condition maintenance	Undecided
Time lag in beyond line of sight scenarios	Undecided
5) What paradigm shifts from our current air-refueling methods must occur to best incorporate the concept of using RPAs as tankers to air-refuel receiver RPAs, considering sound systems engineering techniques as well as the future anti-access / area denial (A2/AD) needs of tomorrow's conflicts?	
Integration of manned and unmanned flight	Strongly Agree
More emphasis on communications and security	Strongly Agree

Standardized transfer method must be adaptable to and inclusive of a wide variety of platforms	Strongly Agree
Change engineering outlook to question a system from design to operation for its <u>intended use</u>	Agree
Develop fully integrated system-of-systems	Agree
Pilot acceptance of RPAs	Agree
Safety standards must meet those of manned aircraft	Agree
RPA AR system must allow for multiple types of fuel	Undecided
Federal Aviation Administration and International Civil Aviation Authority acceptance of RPAs	Undecided
In A2/AD environment, freedom of movement must be maintained to allow for AR	Undecided

A noteworthy point was the consensus on "Undecided" for several ideas. For instance, the ONLY consensus that was found for question four was "Undecided" for three out of the six ideas generated. Thus, the difficulties that need to be addressed early in order to successfully utilize RPAs as tankers to air-refuel receiver RPAs is a clear sticking point among experts that ought to receive attention. A second interesting point is the slight contradiction concerning pilot perception and acceptance of RPAs. In response to question five, the expert panel agreed that pilot acceptance of RPAs is an important paradigm shift necessary to best incorporate the concept of using RPAs as tankers to air-refuel receiver RPAs. Yet, in question three, aviator perception of RPAs was one of the ideas that reached a consensus of "Undecided" as to whether it would be an unavoidable drawback of utilizing RPAs to air-refuel receiver RPAs.

The following ideas shown in Table 7 did not reach consensus:

Table 7. Round Two Non-Consensus Items

Question & Criteria	IQR
1) Which RPA in the current AF inventory could be used to air-refuel future RPAs without major structural changes to the aircraft?	
None	4
Global Hawk	3
Global Hawk (High Speed/High Capacity Variant) & Predator B (Low Speed Variant)	4
2) What advantages are to be gained over manned air-refueling platforms, including new mission sets that could be created, by utilizing RPAs as tankers to air-refuel receiver RPAs?	
Constant ISR presence	3
Elimination of danger to human crews	2
3) What are the unavoidable drawbacks of utilizing RPAs to air-refuel receiver RPAs?	
None	1.75
Control algorithms for formation flying	2
Hijacking risk: enemy assuming complete control of the vehicle	4
Concept of operations	2
4) What difficulties need to be addressed early in prototyping, planning, procurement, or training in order to successfully utilize RPAs as tankers to air-refuel receiver RPAs?	
Interface to provide relative location data for both tanker and receiver	2
Design-in acceptable levels of safety using common engineering practices	2
Cultural challenge: pilots perceive they are "losing their jobs" to machines	2
5) What paradigm shifts from our current air-refueling methods must occur to best incorporate the concept of using RPAs as tankers to air-refuel receiver RPAs, considering sound systems engineering techniques as well as the future anti-access / area denial (A2/AD) needs of tomorrow's conflicts?	
Highly autonomous systems are inevitable and can protect our way of life	2
American service members protect our country with less overseas basing	3
RPA AR system must allow for a wide range of potential flight profiles	2

Of all the questions, the first exhibited the most disagreement between the expert panel in terms of the most number of consistently high IQRs; none of the ideas generated by the expert panel for this question reached consensus in Round Two.

Round Three

The Round Three Questionnaire can be found in Appendix C. In Round Three, three of the five experts on the panel agreed with the ratings of the items that reached group consensus in Round Two. Furthermore, the following five items listed in Table 8 were added to the list of consensus.

Table 8. Round Three Consensus Items

Question & Criteria	Rating
1) Which RPA in the current AF inventory could be used to air-refuel future RPAs without major structural changes to the aircraft?	
Global Hawk	Disagree
Global Hawk (High Speed/High Capacity Variant) & Predator B (Low Speed Variant)	Agree
3) What are the unavoidable drawbacks of utilizing RPAs to air refuel receiver RPAs?	
Concept of operations	Agree
4) What difficulties need to be addressed early in prototyping, planning, procurement, or training in order to successfully utilize RPAs as tankers to air-refuel receiver RPAs?	
Cultural challenge: pilots perceive they are "losing their jobs" to machines	Undecided
5) What paradigm shifts from our current air-refueling methods must occur to best incorporate the concept of using RPAs as tankers to air-refuel receiver RPAs, considering sound systems engineering techniques as well as the future anti-access / area denial (A2/AD) needs of tomorrow's conflicts?	
RPA AR system must allow for a wide range of potential flight profiles	Undecided

Senior Leader Round

The intent of the SL Round was to draw in the opinions of SLs mid-study in a way that minimized time demands while still collecting their critical views on the issue. In coordination with the sponsors of the research, the target audience of the SL Round included the requirements and programming directorates of AMC and ACC, as well as Chief Scientists in various USAF high level research organizations. Major General Woodward graciously sent the questionnaire via email to the personnel identified by the researcher, as well as several other senior leaders she deemed appropriate to participate. The SL Round Questionnaire can be found in Appendix D. Table 9 outlines the level of expertise exhibited by the six SL panel members who responded.

Table 9. Senior Leader Panel Members

MAJCOM Director of Operations
MAJCOM Chief Scientist
MAJCOM A5/8
MAJCOM Senior Executive Service
MAJCOM A3
Retired HAF Deputy CoS for ISR

Table 10 outlines the items that reached consensus in the SL panel using the same criteria as described above with an IQR of one or less. Also depicted in the table is the expert panel's rating of each item for comparison. Items depicted in green indicate a match between the SL and the expert panel, while items in yellow represent a rating on the same side of the scale by the two groups. The SL items that did not match the expert panel's ratings are shown normally.

Table 10. Senior Leader Round Consensus Items

Question	Senior Leaders	Expert Panel
RPAs could serve as tankers to perform the air-refueling mission against receiver RPAs.	Agree	Strongly Agree
1) Which RPA in the current AF inventory could be used to air-refuel future RPAs without major structural changes to the aircraft?		
Global Hawk (High Speed/High Capacity Variant) & Predator B (Low Speed Variant)	Disagree	Agree
2) What advantages are to be gained over manned air-refueling platforms, including new mission sets that could be created, by utilizing RPAs as tankers to air-refuel receiver RPAs?		
Elimination of danger to human crews	Agree	IQR - 2
Availability of enhanced aerodynamics and stealthier shapes	Agree	Agree
3) What are the unavoidable drawbacks are of utilizing RPAs to air refuel receiver RPAs?		
Need to prevent enemy interference (anti-tamper, anti-spoofing) with the vehicle	Agree	Strongly Agree
Technology development	Agree	Agree
Link robustness	Agree	Agree
Lost link protocols	Agree	Agree
Lack of understanding in proper employment of RPAs	Agree	Agree
High cost	Undecided	Undecided
4) What difficulties need to be addressed early in prototyping, planning, procurement, or training in order to successfully utilize RPAs as tankers to air-refuel receiver RPAs?		
Interface to provide relative location data for both tanker and receiver	Agree	IQR - 2
Hand-off between beyond line of sight to line of sight data link systems	Agree	Undecided
Design-in acceptable levels of safety using common engineering practices	Agree	IQR - 2
Develop prognostic health and service life surveillance to enable on-condition maintenance	Agree	Undecided
Cultural challenge: pilots perceive they are "losing their jobs" to	Disagree	Undecided

machines		
5) What paradigm shifts from our current air-refueling methods must occur to best incorporate the concept of using RPAs as tankers to air-refuel receiver RPAs, considering sound systems engineering techniques as well as the future anti-access / area denial (A2/AD) needs of tomorrow's conflicts?		
Highly autonomous systems are inevitable and can protect our way of life	Agree	IQR - 2
Integration of manned and unmanned flight	Agree	Strongly Agree
More emphasis on communications and security	Disagree	Strongly Agree
RPA AR system must allow for multiple types of fuel	Undecided	Undecided
Federal Aviation Administration and International Civil Aviation Authority acceptance of RPAs	Strongly Agree	Undecided
In A2/AD environment, freedom of movement must be maintained to allow for AR	Undecided	Undecided
RPA AR system must allow for a wide range of potential flight profiles	Disagree	Undecided

The SL participants provided a plethora of comments along with their ratings. One SL stated that he was not convinced that the Global Hawk – to – Global Hawk AR demonstration offers any practical operational utility. Still another SL proposed that the idea not be limited to current RPAs, but also envisioned as optionally piloted vehicles or unmanned conventional tanker aircraft; this point is consistent with the idea of the levels of automation on a continuum.

Several contradicting SL comments showed dissonance on the topics of doctrine, culture, cost, FAA and ICAO acceptance, and technological feasibility. With respect to the need for an airpower practitioner to influence the RPA tasking system, one SL asserted that "The challenge will be to ensure RPAs are appropriately integrated into increasingly complex Air Tasking Orders and tasked according to competing mission

73

demands across Combatant Commander boundaries and requirements from various agencies." Another SL commented that this is an "effort that should already be in place."

A variety of comments pertaining to pilot acceptance, aviator perceptions and an associated culture shift were obtained from the SL Round. One SL asserted that he was not concerned so much with aviator perception but with the perception of the general public. Further, he stated the cultural shift required for pilot acceptance would not be too much of a challenge. Another SL avowed that trust in RPAs must be earned and until it is, there would be limitations on mixed manned and unmanned operations. Another maintained that continued use of RPAs would mature perceptions, but this process may take time. One SL offered the opinion that pilot perception may not be a consideration for RPA integration, but could become a "serious AF pilot recruiting issue in the future." In contrast, another SL alleged that general questions about the acceptance of RPAs are "probably stale by about a decade."

There were distinct opposing comments concerning the cost of using RPAs as tankers to air-refuel receiver RPAs. While one SL commented that RPA AR will require extensive funding to advance the technology, another viewed the initiative as a cost savings.

FAA and ICAO acceptance of RPAs was identified by one SL as an area requiring a paradigm shift. Another asserted that relaxing limitations on mixed operations between manned and unmanned vehicles hinged on this acceptance. Finally, another foreshadowed that an FAA/ICAO paradigm shift may soon occur.

There also was a wide range of comments regarding the time lag in beyond line of sight scenarios. One SL affirmed that this concept would be the biggest technological hurdle. Another stated that we cannot rely on beyond-line-of-sight command and control for all functions; some must be local or autonomous. In contrast, another SL confirmed that AFRL's AAR program has already demonstrated this capability for the receiver.

Finally, one of the SLs took the time to offer several valuable insights to the study. He asserted that the study questions contain a generalization that may lead to a faulty or low value set of conclusions due to the combination of three variables into one set of questions that don't permit examination of each of the critical variables. He suggests the following three questions to which he assigned his rating (Table 11):

Table 11. Senior Leader "X" Ratings

Criteria	Rating
Efficacy of an RPA AR platform, vice a manned tanker platform	Strongly Agree
Efficacy of extending RPA loiter time through AR with a manned or unmanned tanker	Strongly Disagree
Efficacy of an unmanned AR platform operating with unmanned receivers	Strongly Disagree

He further suggested narrowing the scope of the research to specifically address acceptance of the following RPA functions (Table 12):

Table 12. RPA Functional Areas

RPAs in the Air-Refueling mission task
RPAs in the Global Integrated ISR core function
RPAs in the Global Precision Attack core function
RPAs in the Air Superiority core function
RPAs in the Global Mobility core function
RPAs in Nuclear Weapons Delivery task

A final point made was that many of the ideas generated by the expert panel were generalizable to the concept of RPAs as a whole, and not specific to RPAs performing the AR mission.

V. Discussion

"We are all pilgrims on the same journey—but some pilgrims have better roadmaps."
- *Nelson DeMille*

The purpose of this study was to frame the RPA AR problem. In essence, its value was as a preliminary "testing of the waters" on the subject. Its aim was to act as a first step in determining what kind of policy, programming, and procurement issues ought to be further fleshed out in future studies on the subject of using RPAs as tanker to air-refuel receiver RPAs. As such, there were generally four different combined expert panel and SL panel outcomes for each of the topics identified. First, some of the items did not reach consensus in either group. Second, some items reached consensus in one group, but not the other. These two categories combined embody those issues where we must raise consciousness and awareness in order to eventually find consensus. The lack of consensus found in the population sampled does not necessarily mean that consensus does not exist in the larger population, but rather that a larger sample size may be required to reveal it.

The third possible outcome was the items where the expert panel disagreed with the SLs. A logical response to these items would be to lean towards trusting SL opinion more on matters of policy while trusting expert opinions more on matters of practice and tactics. For instance, in the case of deciding future policy on FAA/ICAO acceptance of RPAs, I recommend deferring to SLs. Alternatively, in the case of disagreement over the level of emphasis on communications and security, I recommend relying on the experts as the users of the technology.

The final situation was the eight cases where SLs agreed with the expert panel, as shown in Table 13.

Table 13. Eight Areas of Strong Consensus

2) What advantages are to be gained over manned air-refueling platforms, including new mission sets that could be created, by utilizing RPAs as tankers to air-refuel receiver RPAs?		
Availability of enhanced aerodynamics and stealthier shapes	Agree	Agree
3) What are the unavoidable drawbacks are of utilizing RPAs to air refuel receiver RPAs?		
Technology development	Agree	Agree
Link robustness	Agree	Agree
Lost link protocols	Agree	Agree
Lack of understanding in proper employment of RPAs	Agree	Agree
High cost	Undecided	Undecided
5) What paradigm shifts from our current air-refueling methods must occur to best incorporate the concept of using RPAs as tankers to air-refuel receiver RPAs, considering sound systems engineering techniques as well as the future anti-access / area denial (A2/AD) needs of tomorrow's conflicts?		
RPA AR system must allow for multiple types of fuel	Undecided	Undecided
In A2/AD environment, freedom of movement must be maintained to allow for AR	Undecided	Undecided

Conclusions

In sum, both the expert panel and the SLs agreed that RPAs could be used to perform the AR mission against receiver RPAs. The literature review, along with comments made by the expert panel, illustrate that clearly the technology to accomplish this feat does exist. That being said, the researcher's overall impression of the SL opinions was that of reservation; in essence, they confirm that yes, we can do this, but the question of *should* we is yet to be determined.

The question of whether advancements in RPA AR should be pursued is tied to the level of consensus displayed by this study. Of the 43 total ideas generated by the expert panel in Round One, 33 of those, or 76.7%, reached consensus by the end of Round Three. Of those, only 20 ideas, or 46.5%, reached consensus in a direction other than a neutral opinion. In contrast, the SL Round found intersections of consensus on only 10 items, or 23.3%. Of those, only 7 ideas, or 16.3%, found consensus on other than "Undecided." Thus, it appears there exists a significant disagreement between experts and SLs on the way forward for RPA AR. Consistent with research described in the literature review, the military must resolve doctrinal issues to better guide the system engineering process that produces the weapon system. Until this happens, and considering the lack of consensus found by this study, competing methods for extending RPAs may prove more feasible. Considering that this study only polled 11 people out of the plethora of stakeholders involved in this endeavor, the ease of coordination and the reduced complexity of alternative power methods may outweigh the cost of finding consensus on RPA AR.

The following seven areas, however, did reach consensus in a strong direction for SLs and represent agreement that can be capitalized on. Participants agreed that the availability of enhanced aerodynamics and stealthier shapes are a significant advantage over manned AR platforms of utilizing RPAs as tankers to air-refuel receiver RPAs. Further, they agree on the following unavoidable drawbacks of utilizing RPAs to air-refuel receiver RPAs: the need to prevent enemy interference (anti-tamper, anti-spoofing) with the vehicle, technology development, link robustness, lost link protocols, and the lack of understanding in proper employment of RPAs. Finally, they agree that the integration of manned and unmanned flight is an important paradigm shift from current AR methods that must occur to best incorporate the concept of using RPAs as tankers to air-refuel receiver RPAs.

My Dad, an AF and commercial airline pilot of over 40 years, laments as I conduct this research that I am "writing myself out of a job!" I counter his point by asserting that this is exactly the Luddite mentality that must be eliminated in our military's way forward! Luckily, the new generation who will implement RPAs into our military doctrine has been born, and we are taking measures to cultivate its growth. According to the AF Academy Public Affairs Office (2012), a team of four cadets who designed a small RPA dubbed the "Aardvark" traveled to the US Military Academy in early May of 2012. There, they worked with Naval Academy midshipmen and West Point cadets who have designed unmanned surface vehicles and unmanned ground vehicles. Their goal: to track and intercept a target (Branum, 2012). Thus, not only are we cultivating the incorporation of unmanned technology into our military doctrine, but we also are encouraging the abolition of service rivalries early on in military careers.

Limitations of the Study

There are several limitations to this study. First, the study is based on the assumption that using RPAs as tankers to air-refuel receiver RPAs is the optimal method for filling the capability gap presented by the limited range and access issues of today's RPAs. As several SLs pointed out, RPA AR may be technologically feasible, but there is still the question of whether this solution is the optimal one for filling the capability gap. As illuminated in the literature review, there are competing alternatives.

Second, the results are not generalizable for several reasons. The findings of the study can only be attributed to the five experts and six SLs who participated. Due to nonrandom sampling and small sample size, the results are not necessarily statistically significant. The low participation rate contributes to common sampling error such as under-coverage and representation error. As stated previously, the number of stakeholders who ought to be involved in these policy decisions is extraordinary and the resultant coordination required between them to obtain consensus is staggering. Unfortunately, several experts whose opinions would have contributed to the study declined participation. Thus, this research only captured a snippet of those involved in the endeavor. For these reasons, the conclusions drawn from the study are limited to the input from the participating Delphi group members.

Finally, the amount of time and effort required to carry out a Delphi study with even as few people who participated in this study was challenging for a single researcher. With the exception of transmitting and receiving the surveys electronically from respondents, I carried out the process of calculating consensus manually. This point represents an area for improvement in future studies that require the collaboration between numerous stakeholders and the amalgamation of a large collection of ideas.

Future Research

Future research can address the limitation issues just described. First, future research must address the major assumption made in this research. One concept illustrated by this research is the complex coordination required between a plethora of stakeholders in order to properly incorporate RPA AR into military doctrine. While the technology to achieve this goal certainly exists, the complication of managing the change may relegate it as a less feasible option. Good systems engineering demands that we look at other options in solving the RPA limited range and access problem. Thus, RPA AR ought to be weighed in a cost-benefit analysis against other methods for extending RPAs. For instance, more efficient engines or alternative fuels could prove to extend the RPA ISR presence at a less costly price in terms of the complex coordination of all stakeholders involved.

Second, in order for this idea to succeed and become a useful and worthwhile tool for our US military, a critical mass of the stakeholders involved must fully buy-in to further progression in the field. The USAF must lead the way in a coordinated effort that produces a unified voice, unaffected by the stovepipes that traditionally create rivalries between sister services. By boosting participation in a study like this, the statistical significance of the results could be enhanced, thus improving the overall generalization of the consensus found for future policy. Moreover, the Delphi process of rating and continuous feedback to panel members could be streamlined through the use of technology to computerize the rating and consensus calculation portion of the process. This, in turn, would facilitate the ability to allow higher participation with the goal of reducing group error and ultimately boosting decision quality.

Third, a different method for addressing the heavy workload required for the Delphi technique would be the Normative Group Technique (NGT) developed by Delbeq. This methodology is essentially a face-to-face version of the Delphi method. In it, participating members proceed through the following steps: silent idea generation, round-robin sharing of ideas, feedback to the group, explanatory group discussion, individual re-assessment, and finally, a mathematical aggregation of the revised judgments. Ultimately, the NGT produces a prioritized list of ideas in two hours or less (Delbeq, Van de Ven, and Gustafson, 1975). Thus, the NGT method could be utilized in future research to more quickly brainstorm and identify consensus; the reduced amount of time required to accomplish this method may actually boost participation by experts and decision makers who are typically already strapped for time. Additionally, as the study signified a first step into uncharted territory, it represents an area of research ripe for taking to the next level. Building on the issues highlighted by this study, future research should also identify populations that could serve as ready groups for surveying.

A final and more obvious area for future research include those items that both the expert panel and the SLs reached consensus on in the "Undecided" category. These items include: the notion that high cost is an unavoidable drawback of utilizing RPAs to air-refuel receiver RPAs; the paradigm shift that in an A2/AD environment, freedom of movement must be maintained to allow for AR; and the paradigm shift that RPA AR systems must allow for multiple types of fuel.

In summary, the USAF is in desperate need to get back into the game with respect to RPAs and to prove its dedication to the support of our sister services. No one can argue the proven significance of AR throughout its relatively short history. Similarly, the importance of RPAs to modern warfare is par none, yet the USAF has yet to embrace its responsibility in their development and implementation. Further, there exists a plethora of research supporting the technological feasibility of the marriage of AR capability with RPAs. Within the context of the ASBC, this marriage is invaluable to our national security. The N-UCLASS provides the perfect opportunity for the USAF to get back in the game. By getting involved early in the design phase and remaining in close contact throughout the procurement process, the USAF can better assess its customers' requirements. Ultimately, through sound systems engineering techniques and intimate collaboration between all stakeholders, the USAF should provide its customers with a

reengineered service that enhances the protection of our great nation.

Glossary

AAF	Army Air Force
AAR	Automated Air-Refueling
AARD	Autonomous Airborne Refueling Demonstration
ACC	Air Combat Command
ACTD	Advanced Concept Technology Demonstration
AF	Air Force
AFB	Air Force Base
AFCoS	Air Force Chief of Staff
AFIT	Air Force Institute of Technology
AFRICOM	Africa Command
AFRL	Air Force Research Laboratory
AMC	Air Mobility Command
AMMP	Air Mobility Master Plan
AOR	Area of Responsibility
AR	Air-Refueling
ASBC	AirSea Battle Concept
A2/AD	Anti-Access / Area Denial
CENTAF	Central Command Air Forces
CENTCOM	Central Command
COA	Certificate of Authorization
CVN	Nuclear Aircraft Carrier
DARPA	Defense Advanced Research Projects Agency
DoD	Department of Defense
FAA	Federal Aviation Administration
FAR	Federal Aviation Regulation
FEMA	Federal Emergency Management Agency
GPS	Global Positioning System
HAF	Headquarters Air Force
HQ	Headquarters
INCOSE	International Council on Systems Engineering
IQR	Inter-Quartile Range
IRB	Institutional Review Board
ISR	Intelligence, Surveillance and Reconnaissance
JAPCC	Joint Air Power Competence Centre
JCA	Joint Capability Area
J-UCAS	Joint Unmanned Combat Aircraft System
MAJCOM	Major Command
MATS	Military Air Transport Command
MV	Machine Vision
NAS	National Air Space
NASA	National Aeronautics and Space Administration

NATO	North Atlantic Treaty Organization
N-UCLASS	Navy Unmanned Carrier Launched Airborne Surveillance and Strike System
PACOM	Pacific Command
PAF	Project Air Force
OCS	Operator Control Station
QDR	Quadrennial Defense Review
RAND	Research and Development
RPA	Remotely Piloted Aircraft
RSO	Remote Split Operations
SAB	Scientific Advisory Board
SAC	Strategic Air Command
SECAF	Secretary of the Air Force
SECDEF	Secretary of Defense
SECNAV	Secretary of the Navy
SES	Senior Executive Service
STANAG	Standardization Agreement
UAS	Unmanned Aerial System
UAV	Unmanned Aerial Vehicle
UCAV	Unmanned Combat Air Vehicle
USAAS	United States Army Air Service
USAF	United States Air Force
USN	United States Navy
WWI	World War I
WWII	World War II

**Remotely Piloted Aircraft (RPA) Performing the Air-Refueling Mission Delphi Study
Questionnaire**

Thank you for agreeing to participate in this Delphi Study. The purpose of this research is to determine, as judged by a panel of knowledgeable experts in this area, **the feasibility of using RPAs as tankers to air-refuel receiver RPAs.** The sponsors for this research are Dr. Donald E. Erbschloe, Air Mobility Command Chief Scientist, as well as Major General Margaret H. Woodward, Commander, 17th Air Force and U.S. Air Forces Africa.

Please note the following:

Benefits and risks: There are no personal benefits or risks for participating in this survey. Your participation in the brief survey should take less than 30 minutes per round.

Confidentiality: Your responses are completely confidential, and your identity will remain anonymous. No individual data will be reported; only data in aggregate will be made public. Data will be kept electronically on my government issued laptop. I understand that the names and associated data I collect must be protected at all times, only be known to the researcher, and managed according to the Air Force Institute of Technology (AFIT) interview protocol. All interview data will only be handled by me. At the conclusion of the study, all data will be turned over to the advisor and all other copies will be destroyed. If you have any questions or concerns about your participation in this study, please contact:

SARAH R. LYNCH, Major, USAF IDE Student, Advanced Study of Air Mobility USAF Expeditionary Center JB McGuire-Dix-Lakehurst, NJ DSN 312-650-7750 Comm XXX-XXX-XXXX	ALAN R. HEMINGER, Ph.D. Associate Professor of Management Information Systems Graduate School of Engineering and Management Air Force Institute of Technology Wright-Patterson AFB, OH Voice: 937-255-3636 (785-3636 DSN) ext 7405

Voluntary consent: Your participation is completely voluntary. You have the right to decline to answer any question, as well as refuse to participate in this survey or to withdraw at any time. Your decision of whether or not to participate will not result in any penalty or loss of benefits to which you are otherwise entitled. Completion of the survey implies your consent to participate.

Adverse impact statement: If a subject's future response reasonably places them at risk of criminal or civil liability or is damaging to their financial standing, employability, or reputation, I understand that I am required to immediately file an adverse event report with the AFIT Institutional Review Board office.

Background: Because each respondent will have a different perspective, allow me to give a brief overview of the topic of study.

RPAs are growing both in number of platforms and importance to the USAF operational mission. The ability to refuel these platforms in the air could well be a game-changer. Within the military mindset, the concept of using of RPAs as tankers to air-refuel receiver RPAs is still in its infancy; yet the technological capability does exist commercially. The purpose of this study is to acquire insight and recommendations from subject matter experts and senior leaders on options and methodology to procure this capability. Thank you for participating in this study. I appreciate your time and candid responses.

Process:

1. Please complete this questionnaire **electronically** and return it to: **sarah.lynch@us.af.mil** no later than **13 February 2012.** If you have questions, I can be reached at XXX-XXX-XXXX or via DSN 650-7750.

2. This questionnaire is an instrument of a Delphi Study. The Delphi method is an iterative, group communication process which is used to collect and distill the judgments of experts using a series of questionnaires interspersed with feedback. The questionnaires are designed to focus on problems, opportunities, solutions, or forecasts. *It is critical in the Delphi process that panel members refrain from discussing the study with each other until research is concluded!* Each questionnaire is developed based on the results of the previous questionnaire. The process continues until the research question is answered. For example, when consensus is reached, sufficient information has been exchanged. This usually takes, on average, 3-4 rounds.

3. There are five background questions and five primary questions for this round. The background questions are requested to establish your particular expertise for the study and will not be shared specifically in the report. Again, the survey is non-attribution, so please elaborate fully on your answers. Once all survey responses are received and analyzed, you will be asked to review and revise your initial responses to questions 4 and 5 based on responses provided by the entire group. Subsequent rounds will be announced as needed and all research will conclude by 31 April 2012.

Background questions:
1. Personal Information:
       a. Name:
       b. Rank/Grade:
       c. Current Duty Title:
       d. Time in Current Duty Position:
       e. Core AFSC/MOS/Primary Duty Code:

2. How many total years have you served on a staff above base/wing-level?

3. How many total years have you worked (been involved with) air-refueling or RPA issues? Please specify air-refueling or RPA and if both, please provide separate times for each.

4. Considering all of your staff roles, in what capacities have you dealt with air-refueling or RPA issues? Please specify whether you answer is with respect to air-refueling, RPA or both.

5. On a scale from 1 to 5 (1-strongly disagree, 3-neither agree/disagree, 5-strongly agree), please assess the statement, "RPAs could serve as tankers to perform the air-refueling mission against receiver RPAs." Please elaborate on your response.

Please answer and elaborate on the following questions:

6. Which RPA in the current AF inventory could be used to air-refuel future RPAs without major structural changes to the aircraft?

7. What are the advantages to be gained over manned air-refueling platforms, including new mission sets that could be created, by utilizing RPAs as tankers to air-refuel receiver RPAs?

8. What are the unavoidable drawbacks of utilizing RPAs to air refuel receiver RPAs?

9. What are the difficulties that need to be addressed early in prototyping, planning, procurement, or training in order to successfully utilize RPAs as tankers to air-refuel receiver RPAs?

10. What paradigm shifts from our current air-refueling methods must occur to best incorporate the concept of using RPAs as tankers to air-refuel receiver RPAs, considering sound systems engineering techniques as well as the future anti-access / area denial needs of tomorrow's conflicts?

Appendix B. Round Two

Remotely Piloted Aircraft (RPA) Performing the Air-Refueling Mission Delphi Study
Questionnaire

Thank you for agreeing to participate in this Delphi Study. The purpose of this research is to determine, as judged by a panel of knowledgeable experts in this area, **the feasibility of using RPAs as tankers to air-refuel receiver RPAs.** The sponsors for this research are Dr. Donald E. Erbschloe, Air Mobility Command Chief Scientist, as well as Major General Margaret H. Woodward, Commander, 17th Air Force and U.S. Air Forces Africa.

Please note the following:

<u>Benefits and risks</u>: There are no personal benefits or risks for participating in this survey. Your participation in the brief survey should take less than 30 minutes per round.

<u>Confidentiality</u>: Your responses are completely confidential, and your identity will remain anonymous. No individual data will be reported; only data in aggregate will be made public. Data will be kept electronically on my government issued laptop. I understand that the names and associated data I collect must be protected at all times, only be known to the researcher, and managed according to the Air Force Institute of Technology (AFIT) interview protocol. All interview data will only be handled by me. At the conclusion of the study, all data will be turned over to the advisor and all other copies will be destroyed. If you have any questions or concerns about your participation in this study, please contact:

SARAH R. LYNCH, Major, USAF IDE Student, Advanced Study of Air Mobility USAF Expeditionary Center JB McGuire-Dix-Lakehurst, NJ DSN 312-650-7750 Comm XXX-XXX-XXXX	ALAN R. HEMINGER, Ph.D. Associate Professor of Management Information Systems Graduate School of Engineering and Management Air Force Institute of Technology Wright-Patterson AFB, OH Voice: 937-255-3636 (785-3636 DSN) ext 7405

<u>Voluntary consent</u>: Your participation is completely voluntary. You have the right to decline to answer any question, as well as refuse to participate in this survey or to withdraw at any time. Your decision of whether or not to participate will not result in any penalty or loss of benefits to which you are otherwise entitled. Completion of the survey implies your consent to participate.

<u>Adverse impact statement</u>: If a subject's future response reasonably places them at risk of criminal or civil liability or is damaging to their financial standing, employability, or reputation, I understand that I am required to immediately file an adverse event report with the AFIT Institutional Review Board office.

Background: Because each respondent will have a different perspective, allow me to give a brief overview of the topic of study.

RPAs are growing both in number of platforms and importance to the USAF operational mission. The ability to refuel these platforms in the air could well be a game-changer. Within the military mindset, the concept of using of RPAs as tankers to air-refuel receiver RPAs is still in its infancy; yet the technological capability does exist commercially. The purpose of this study is to acquire insight and recommendations from subject matter experts and senior leaders on options and methodology to procure this capability. Thank you for participating in this study. I appreciate your time and candid responses.

Process:

1. Please complete this questionnaire **electronically** and return it to: **sarah.lynch@us.af.mil** no later than **12 March 2012.** If you have questions, I can be reached at XXX-XXX-XXXX or via DSN 650-7750.

2. This questionnaire is an instrument of a Delphi Study. The Delphi method is an iterative, group communication process which is used to collect and distill the judgments of experts using a series of questionnaires interspersed with feedback. The questionnaires are designed to focus on problems, opportunities, solutions, or forecasts. *It is critical in the Delphi process that panel members refrain from discussing the study with each other until research is concluded!* Each questionnaire is developed based on the results of the previous questionnaire. The process continues until the research question is answered. For example, when consensus is reached, sufficient information has been exchanged. This usually takes, on average, 3-4 rounds.

3. This is **Round #2** of the study. Once all questionnaire responses are received and analyzed, you will be asked to review and revise your initial responses based on collective responses provided by the entire group. Subsequent rounds will be announced as needed and all research will conclude by 6 April 2012.

Questionnaire #2: Rank Order Criteria

Directions:

Using a 5-point Likert Scale, rate the following common themes obtained from the group's answers to each question.

5 = Strongly Agree
4 = Agree
3 = Undecided
2 = Disagree
1 = Strongly Disagree

1) Please review each of the following items identified in Questionnaire #1 for which RPA in the current AF inventory could be used to air-refuel future RPAs without major structural changes to the aircraft?

Criteria	Likert Rating	Comments (agree/disagree/clarify)
None		
Global Hawk		
Global Hawk (High Speed/High Capacity Variant) & Predator B (Low Speed Variant)		

2) Please review each of the following items identified in Questionnaire #1 for what the advantages are to be gained over manned air-refueling platforms, including new mission sets that could be created, by utilizing RPAs as tankers to air-refuel receiver RPAs?

Criteria	Likert Rating	Comments (agree/disagree/clarify)
More efficient use of low density, high demand assets		
Constant ISR presence		
Longer loiter times		
Elimination of danger to human crews		
Availability of enhanced aerodynamics and stealthier shapes		
Reduced AR on-load times due to more reliable rejoins, contacts, and station keeping		

3) Please review each of the following items identified in Questionnaire #1 for what the unavoidable drawbacks are of utilizing RPAs to air refuel receiver RPAs?

Criteria	Likert Rating	Comments (agree/disagree/clarify)
None		
Technology development		
Reliability, consistency, and operational readiness		
Control algorithms for formation flying		
Link robustness		
Need to prevent enemy interference (anti-tamper, anti-spoofing) with the vehicle		
Lost link protocols		
Contingency management		
Hijacking risk: enemy assuming complete control of the vehicle		
High cost		
Aviator perception of RPAs		
Lack of understanding in proper employment of RPAs		

	Likert Rating	Comments (agree/disagree/clarify)
Need for an airpower practitioner to influence RPA tasking system		
Concept of operations		
Bed-down and maintenance		

4) Please review each of the following items identified in Questionnaire #1 for what the difficulties are that need to be addressed early in prototyping, planning, procurement, or training in order to successfully utilize RPAs as tankers to air-refuel receiver RPAs?

Criteria	Likert Rating	Comments (agree/disagree/clarify)
Interface to provide relative location data for both tanker and receiver		
Time lag in beyond line of sight scenarios		
Hand-off between beyond line of sight to line of sight data link systems		
Design-in acceptable levels of safety using common engineering practices		
Cultural challenge: pilots perceive they are "losing their jobs" to machines		
Develop prognostic health and service life surveillance to enable on-condition maintenance		

5) Please review each of the following items identified in Questionnaire #1 for what paradigm shifts from our current air-refueling methods must occur to best incorporate the concept of using RPAs as tankers to air-refuel receiver RPAs, considering sound systems engineering techniques as well as the future anti-access / area denial (A2/AD) needs of tomorrow's conflicts?

Criteria	Likert Rating	Comments (agree/disagree/clarify)
Highly autonomous systems are inevitable and can protect our way of life		
American service members protect our country with less overseas basing		
Change engineering outlook to question a system from design to operation for its intended use		
Develop fully integrated system-of-systems		
Federal Aviation Administration and International Civil Aviation Authority acceptance of RPAs		
Integration of manned and unmanned flight		

Pilot acceptance of RPAs		
More emphasis on communications and security		
Safety standards must meet those of manned aircraft		
In A2/AD environment, freedom of movement must be maintained to allow for AR		
Standardized transfer method must be adaptable to and inclusive of a wide variety of platforms		
RPA AR system must allow for multiple types of fuel		
RPA AR system must allow for a wide range of potential flight profiles		

Appendix C. Round Three

Remotely Piloted Aircraft (RPA) Performing the Air-Refueling Mission Delphi Study Questionnaire

Thank you for agreeing to participate in this Delphi Study. The purpose of this research is to determine, as judged by a panel of knowledgeable experts in this area, **the feasibility of using RPAs as tankers to air-refuel receiver RPAs.** The sponsors for this research are Dr. Donald E. Erbschloe, Air Mobility Command Chief Scientist, as well as Major General Margaret H. Woodward, Commander, 17th Air Force and U.S. Air Forces Africa.

Please note the following:

<u>Benefits and risks</u>: There are no personal benefits or risks for participating in this survey. Your participation in the brief survey should take less than 30 minutes per round.

<u>Confidentiality</u>: Your responses are completely confidential, and your identity will remain anonymous. No individual data will be reported; only data in aggregate will be made public. Data will be kept electronically on my government issued laptop. I understand that the names and associated data I collect must be protected at all times, only be known to the researcher, and managed according to the Air Force Institute of Technology (AFIT) interview protocol. All interview data will only be handled by me. At the conclusion of the study, all data will be turned over to the advisor and all other copies will be destroyed. If you have any questions or concerns about your participation in this study, please contact:

SARAH R. LYNCH, Major, USAF IDE Student, Advanced Study of Air Mobility USAF Expeditionary Center JB McGuire-Dix-Lakehurst, NJ DSN 312-650-7750 Comm XXX-XXX-XXXX	ALAN R. HEMINGER, Ph.D. Associate Professor of Management Information Systems Graduate School of Engineering and Management Air Force Institute of Technology Wright-Patterson AFB, OH Voice: 937-255-3636 (785-3636 DSN) ext 7405

<u>Voluntary consent</u>: Your participation is completely voluntary. You have the right to decline to answer any question, as well as refuse to participate in this survey or to withdraw at any time. Your decision of whether or not to participate will not result in any penalty or loss of benefits to which you are otherwise entitled. Completion of the survey implies your consent to participate.

<u>Adverse impact statement</u>: If a subject's future response reasonably places them at risk of criminal or civil liability or is damaging to their financial standing, employability, or reputation, I understand that I am required to immediately file an adverse event report with the AFIT Institutional Review Board office.

Background: Because each respondent will have a different perspective, allow me to give a brief overview of the topic of study.

RPAs are growing both in number of platforms and importance to the USAF operational mission. The ability to refuel these platforms in the air could well be a game-changer. Within the military mindset, the concept of using of RPAs as tankers to air-refuel receiver RPAs is still in its infancy; yet the technological capability does exist commercially. The purpose of this study is to acquire insight and recommendations from subject matter experts and senior leaders on options and methodology to procure this capability. Thank you for participating in this study. I appreciate your time and candid responses.

Process:

1. Please complete this questionnaire **electronically** and return it to: **sarah.lynch@us.af.mil** no later than **6 April 2012.** If you have questions, I can be reached at XXX-XXX-XXXX or via DSN 650-7750.

2. This questionnaire is an instrument of a Delphi Study. The Delphi method is an iterative, group communication process which is used to collect and distill the judgments of experts using a series of questionnaires interspersed with feedback. The questionnaires are designed to focus on problems, opportunities, solutions, or forecasts. *It is critical in the Delphi process that panel members refrain from discussing the study with each other until research is concluded!* Each questionnaire is developed based on the results of the previous questionnaire. The process continues until the research question is answered. For example, when consensus is reached, sufficient information has been exchanged. This usually takes, on average, 3-4 rounds.

3. This is the **3rd and FINAL round** of the Delphi study. Once all questionnaire responses are received, an analysis of the Round 3 results will be conducted and the results will be summarized and sent to you in a final report.

Questionnaire #3

Part 1 – Results from Questionnaire #2

Below are the results from questionnaire #2. Based on the group's ratings, **consensus was reached on 0 criteria** for the first research question, **4 criteria** for the second research question, **11 criteria** for the third research question, **3 criteria** for the fourth research questions, and **10 criteria** for the fifth research question. The criteria below were listed in order based on the arithmetic median and inter-quartile range (the range that contains the answers of the middle 50 percent of the respondents) of the group's responses. For this study, an inter-quartile range (IQR) of 1 or less is an indicator of consensus.

Directions:

First, **review the ratings in the middle columns for each research**. Then, **select "Yes" or "No" in box below.** If you select "yes," then you are finished with this section. If you select "No," please re-rank and comment as needed. Be sure to use the same 5-point rating scale from the last round. Once completed, **continue on to Part 2.**

I agree with ratings as determined by the group in Round 2:

Yes (Proceed to part 2)	
No (Re-rank, comment, then proceed to Part 2)	

2) What advantages are to be gained over manned air-refueling platforms, including new mission sets that could be created, by utilizing RPAs as tankers to air-refuel receiver RPAs?

5 = Strongly Agree, 4 = Agree, 3 = Undecided, 2 = Disagree, 1 = Strongly Disagree

Criteria	Your Rating	Grp Med	Grp IQR	Comments (agree/disagree/clarify)	New Rating/Comment
Longer loiter times		5	1	- Only an advantage in the form of reduced maintenance due to reduced T/O and landings. - Again, difficult with manned or conventional RPAs.	
Availability of enhanced aerodynamics and stealthier shapes		4	0	- Definitely an advantage. - The elimination of aircrew would facilitate that but the two aircraft still need to rendezvous. Some kind of temporary stealth compromising communications have to be used for that.	
Reduced AR on-load times due to more reliable rejoins, contacts, and station keeping		4	0	- Not as key as others above.	
More efficient use of low density, high demand assets		4	1	- Air Refueling equipment is weight that will be added to the airframe that will raise costs and lower total payload.	

97

3) What are the unavoidable drawbacks are of utilizing RPAs to air refuel receiver RPAs?

5 = Strongly Agree, 4 = Agree, 3 = Undecided, 2 = Disagree, 1 = Strongly Disagree

Criteria	Your Rating	Grp Med	Grp IQR	Comments (agree/disagree/clarify)	New Rating/Comment
Need to prevent enemy interference (anti-tamper, anti-spoofing) with the vehicle		5	1	- This can be addressed at low risk with SAASM GPS receivers and existing GPS Anti-Jam technology; however it is relatively expensive today. But jamming and spoofing can be detected, although their presence can potentially prevent the refueling operation. - Big.	
Technology development		4	0	- I believe the technology is relatively mature, TRL 6 now, TRL 7 soon. - The technology exists; it just needs to be adapted.	
Link robustness		4	0	- Not difficult to design to a specified level of continuity and availability into a link. Also, nav algorithms can be designed to take lost data packets into account while preserving safety. - Stealth vs Comms.	
Lost link protocols		4	0	- Not a significant issue, can be defined using conventional engineering practices	
Contingency management		4	1	- Not a significant issue, can be defined using conventional engineering practices	
Lack of understanding in proper employment of RPAs		4	1	- This can be mitigated by investing in proper definition of system requirements and CONOPS. - We started flying UAVs in Vietnam; We have yet to take them seriously.	
Aviator perception of RPAs		3	1	- Agree-have to make the owners and users of manned airspace comfortable with RPAs. Answer is redundant fail-operational RPA navigation and control	

				systems (and associated safety assessments numerically verifying a sufficiently low level of risk). Then acceptance will come with many hours of demonstrated safe operations. - An RPA can have a crew of 10 and still outmaneuver any threat.	
Need for an airpower practitioner to influence RPA tasking system		3	1	- Not certain who airpower practitioner is-again can be mitigated ahead of time with proper CONOPS defining roles of all operational stakeholders, and proper training.	
Reliability, consistency, and operational readiness		3	1	- These are items that can be addressed with conventional engineering processes.	- This completely depends on the operation design constrains of the aircraft, the theater it is operated in, and its budget.

4) What difficulties need to be addressed early in prototyping, planning, procurement, or training in order to successfully utilize RPAs as tankers to air-refuel receiver RPAs?
5 = Strongly Agree, 4 = Agree, 3 = Undecided, 2 = Disagree, 1 = Strongly Disagree

Criteria	Your Rating	Grp Med	Grp IQR	Comments (agree/disagree/clarify)	New Rating/Comment
Hand-off between beyond line of sight to line of sight data link systems		3	0	- Same reason as above, no reason for real-time command and control or monitoring, so hand- off from "beyond line of sight" to "line of sight" data link systems are not relevant to the refueling operation. - Not hard.	
Develop prognostic health and service life surveillance to enable on-condition maintenance		3	0	- This is key, the life cycle cost of these systems must be quantified from the beginning, with built in test, etc built in to minimize the cost of supporting ground personnel.	
Time lag in beyond line of sight scenarios		3	1	- The refueling operation can be designed to be autonomous, and not require real-time remote monitoring of the operation to remain safe. So I see no issues with time lag. - Most of the Lag is due analog to digital to analog translators, not distance. With good hardware this can almost be eliminated.	

5) What paradigm shifts from our current air-refueling methods must occur to best incorporate the concept of using RPAs as tankers to air-refuel receiver RPAs, considering sound systems engineering techniques as well as the future anti-access / area denial (A2/AD) needs of tomorrow's conflicts?

5 = Strongly Agree, 4 = Agree, 3 = Undecided, 2 = Disagree, 1 = Strongly Disagree

Criteria	Your Rating	Grp Med	Grp IQR	Comments (agree/disagree/clarify)	New Rating/Comment
Integration of manned and unmanned flight		5	1	- Very important for airspace access.	
More emphasis on communications and security		5	1		
Standardized transfer method must be adaptable to and inclusive of a wide variety of platforms		5	1		
Change engineering outlook to question a system from design to operation for its intended use		4	1	- Have users with former air-refueling and UAV experience that can monitor the design process.	
Develop fully integrated system-of-systems		4	1		
Pilot acceptance of RPAs		4	1		
Safety standards must meet those of manned aircraft		4	1	- Very important to gain airspace access and to ensure safe operations to gain acceptance. - There are different design safety concerns for both. For example, crew chiefs interface with the aircraft for ground ops (UAV vehicle power, control check, engine start, etc).	
RPA AR system must allow for multiple types of fuel		3	0	- I think all RPAs are moving towards standard heavy fuel, even piston powered machines. - KC-10 is capable of this.	
Federal Aviation Administration and International Civil Aviation Authority acceptance of RPAs		3	1	- Very important, but must also include use in military manned airspace. - It will happen. UPS is already looking at unmanned Transports.	
In A2/AD environment, freedom of movement must be maintained to allow for AR		3	1	- An unmanned A/R capability would contribute to mitigating an A2/AD environment.	

Part 2 - Reviewing and Re-rating the Remaining Criteria

The items below **did not** reach consensus in the last round. Therefore, these items for research questions 1 through 5 should be reviewed and re-assessed by the group in an effort to reach consensus.

Directions:

Please **re-rate**, the criteria for each research question by your agreement at this time, considering the group median rating and comments. Use the same 1-5 scale below. Add comments as needed for clarification.

1) Which RPA in the current AF inventory could be used to air-refuel future RPAs without major structural changes to the aircraft?
5 = Strongly Agree, 4 = Agree, 3 = Undecided, 2 = Disagree, 1 = Strongly Disagree

Criteria	Your Rating	Grp Med	Grp IQR	Comments (agree/disagree/clarify)	New Rating/Comment
None		3	4	- This is currently being proven on the KQ-X program (DARPA). - Attack/ISR aircraft are designed for that roll. They are far from being optimized as a tanker. Check out the KA-6D. It was a good compromise, but it was also designed to carry its weight in bombs.	
Global Hawk		2	3	- Global Hawk operating altitude would be too high for any practical air refueling of tactical assets. Additionally, fuel offload capacity would be very limited for any practical use. - This is currently being proven on the KQ-X program (DARPA). - Concept proving only.	
Global Hawk (High Speed/High Capacity Variant) & Predator B (Low Speed Variant)		4	4	- More complete coverage of potential receivers - Global Hawk operating altitude would be too high for any practical air refueling of tactical assets. Additionally, fuel offload capacity would be very limited for any practical use. - This covers both high and lower speed variants. - Global Hawk is decent for refueling jet powered UAVs due to high speeds. Pred. B is not good. (It would need redesign to increase fuel payload and most likely an off center refueling basket/probe).	

2) What advantages are to be gained over manned air-refueling platforms, including new mission sets that could be created, by utilizing RPAs as tankers to air-refuel receiver RPAs?

5 = Strongly Agree, 4 = Agree, 3 = Undecided, 2 = Disagree, 1 = Strongly Disagree

Criteria	Your Rating	Grp Med	Grp IQR	Comments (agree/disagree/clarify)	New Rating/Comment
Constant ISR presence		4	3	- Already have this – AAR just makes it easier. - Very important-something hard to do with manned A/C. - Is already done using small relatively cheap UAVs that are swapped out at Bingo.	
Elimination of danger to human crews		4	2	- Agree-but not as vital as those above.	

3) What are the unavoidable drawbacks are of utilizing RPAs to air refuel receiver RPAs?

5 = Strongly Agree, 4 = Agree, 3 = Undecided, 2 = Disagree, 1 = Strongly Disagree

Criteria	Your Rating	Grp Med	Grp IQR	Comments (agree/disagree/clarify)	New Rating/Comment
None		5	1.75	- It is a good niche to have for a future battlefield.	
Control algorithms for formation flying		4	2	- I believe this technology is TRL7 except for very small RPAs, SNC has demonstrated on F/A-18/Boeing 707 tanker, on Sikorsky Blackhawk Helos, and soon on KQ-X Global Hawks. - Already done. An F-18 flight test was done showing station keeping was accurate to within 10cm (see link below). Applications to UAV air refueling were noted.	
Hijacking risk: enemy assuming complete control of the vehicle		3	4	- Very unlikely-spoofing can be cross checked and detected with simple aircraft position velocity monitors, command and control links can be encrypted preventing unauthorized control. (Iran's spoofing claims regarding the RQ-170 are highly suspect; even if true it is possible to build in spoofing detection). - I have had people over power and fly my RC planes. UAVs are not much different.	
Concept of operations		4	2	- I believe these can be defined well through standard engineering practices at low risk.	

4) What difficulties need to be addressed early in prototyping, planning, procurement, or training in order to successfully utilize RPAs as tankers to air-refuel receiver RPAs?
5 = Strongly Agree, 4 = Agree, 3 = Undecided, 2 = Disagree, 1 = Strongly Disagree

Criteria	Your Rating	Grp Med	Grp IQR	Comments (agree/disagree/clarify)	New Rating/Comment
Interface to provide relative location data for both tanker and receiver		4	2	- This technology exists and has been proven by Sierra Nevada Corp.	
Design-in acceptable levels of safety using common engineering practices		4	2	- This must be addressed from the first day of the development.	
Cultural challenge: pilots perceive they are "losing their jobs" to machines		2	2	- I think this will come with time, but we need to build in autonomous operation from the beginning and eliminate as much as possible manual operations by pilots and operators.	

5) What paradigm shifts from our current air-refueling methods must occur to best incorporate the concept of using RPAs as tankers to air-refuel receiver RPAs, considering sound systems engineering techniques as well as the future anti-access / area denial (A2/AD) needs of tomorrow's conflicts?
5 = Strongly Agree, 4 = Agree, 3 = Undecided, 2 = Disagree, 1 = Strongly Disagree

Criteria	Your Rating	Grp Med	Grp IQR	Comments (agree/disagree/clarify)	New Rating/Comment
Highly autonomous systems are inevitable and can protect our way of life		4	2	- They are inevitable, but protect is relative to who controls it. **ALL** computers are hack-able no matter what A2/AD you have.	
American service members protect our country with less overseas basing		4	3	- Already do.	
RPA AR system must allow for a wide range of potential flight profiles		4	2	- Slow fight profiles will most likely be using 100LL and faster ones will be using JP-8.	

Appendix D. Senior Leader Round

Remotely Piloted Aircraft (RPA) Performing the Air-Refueling Mission Delphi Study
Senior Leader Questionnaire

Thank you for agreeing to participate in this Delphi Study. The purpose of this research is to determine, as judged by a panel of knowledgeable experts and senior leaders, **the feasibility of using RPAs as tankers to air-refuel receiver RPAs.** The sponsors for this research are Dr. Donald E. Erbschloe, Air Mobility Command Chief Scientist, as well as Major General Margaret H. Woodward, Commander, 17th Air Force and U.S. Air Forces Africa.

Please note the following:

Benefits and risks: There are no personal benefits or risks for participating in this survey. Your participation in the brief survey should take less than 10 minutes.

Confidentiality: Your responses are completely confidential, and your identity will remain anonymous. No individual data will be reported; only data in aggregate will be made public. Data will be kept electronically on my government issued laptop. I understand that the names and associated data I collect must be protected at all times, only be known to the researcher, and managed according to the Air Force Institute of Technology (AFIT) interview protocol. All interview data will only be handled by me. At the conclusion of the study, all data will be turned over to the advisor and all other copies will be destroyed. If you have any questions or concerns about your participation in this study, please contact:

SARAH R. LYNCH, Major, USAF IDE Student, Advanced Study of Air Mobility USAF Expeditionary Center JB McGuire-Dix-Lakehurst, NJ DSN 312-650-7750 Comm XXX-XXX-XXXX	ALAN R. HEMINGER, Ph.D. Associate Professor of Management Information Systems Graduate School of Engineering and Management Air Force Institute of Technology Wright-Patterson AFB, OH Voice: 937-255-3636 (785-3636 DSN) ext 7405

Voluntary consent: Your participation is completely voluntary. You have the right to decline to answer any question, as well as refuse to participate in this survey or to withdraw at any time. Your decision of whether or not to participate will not result in any penalty or loss of benefits to which you are otherwise entitled. Completion of the survey implies your consent to participate.

Adverse impact statement: If a subject's future response reasonably places them at risk of criminal or civil liability or is damaging to their financial standing, employability, or reputation, I understand that I am required to immediately file an adverse event report with the AFIT Institutional Review Board office.

Background: Because each respondent will have a different perspective, allow me to give a brief overview of the topic of study.

RPAs are growing both in number of platforms and importance to the USAF operational mission. The ability to refuel these platforms in the air could well be a game-changer. Within the military mindset, the concept of using of RPAs as tankers to air-refuel receiver RPAs is still in its infancy; yet the technological capability does exist commercially. The purpose of this study is to acquire insight and recommendations from subject matter experts and senior leaders on options and methodology to procure this capability. Thank you for participating in this study. I appreciate your time and candid responses.

Process:

1. Please complete this questionnaire **electronically** and return it to: sarah.lynch@us.af.mil. In order for your input to be properly analyzed, please return it no later than **30 March 2012.** If you have questions, Maj Lynch can also be reached at XXX-XXX-XXXX or via DSN 650-7750.

2. This questionnaire is an instrument of a Delphi Study. The Delphi method is an iterative, group communication process which is used to collect and distill the judgments of experts using a series of questionnaires interspersed with feedback. The questionnaires are designed to focus on problems, opportunities, solutions, or forecasts. *It is critical in the Delphi process that panel members refrain from discussing the study with each other until research is concluded!* Each questionnaire is developed based on the results of the previous questionnaire. The process continues until the research question is answered. For example, when consensus is reached, sufficient information has been exchanged. This usually takes, on average, 3-4 rounds. All research will conclude by 6 April 2012.

3. This particular questionnaire is a separate round of the primary Delphi study intended to capture senior leader perspectives on the use of RPAs as tankers to air-refuel receiver RPAs. It is derived from the first round of the parent study in which a panel of five RPA experts is currently participating in. It consists of the same questions asked of the expert panel and the criteria shown below were generated from the experts' responses in round one. This special round targeting senior leaders will be administered only once; there will be no subsequent rounds. Please note that questions are labeled as pertaining to programming, requirements, or both; please answer those pertaining to your duty position (A3 or A8), but do not hesitate to answer those outside your current job title if you feel your previous experience warrants doing so.

Senior Leader Questionnaire: Rating Criteria

Directions:

Use the following 5-point Likert Rating Scale for each question. The first question is a stand-alone question with one statement to rate, while the following five questions include the themes generated by the expert panel for rating.

5 = Strongly Agree
4 = Agree
3 = Undecided
2 = Disagree
1 = Strongly Disagree

1) (All) Please assess the following statement using the above rating scale, and feel free to elaborate on your response:

Criteria	Likert Rating	Comments (agree/disagree/clarify)
RPAs could serve as tankers to perform the air-refueling mission against receiver RPAs		

2) (Requirements) Please review each of the following items identified by the expert panel for which RPA in the current AF inventory could be used to air-refuel future RPAs without major structural changes to the aircraft?

Criteria	Likert Rating	Comments (agree/disagree/clarify)
None		
Global Hawk		
Global Hawk (High Speed/High Capacity Variant) & Predator B (Low Speed Variant)		

3) (Programming) Please review each of the following items identified by the expert panel for what advantages are to be gained over manned air-refueling platforms, including new mission sets that could be created, by utilizing RPAs as tankers to air-refuel receiver RPAs?

Criteria	Likert Rating	Comments (agree/disagree/clarify)
More efficient use of low density, high demand assets		
Constant ISR presence		
Longer loiter times		
Elimination of danger to human crews		
Availability of enhanced aerodynamics and stealthier shapes		
Reduced AR on-load times due to more reliable rejoins, contacts, and station keeping		

4) (Programming) Please review each of the following items identified by the expert panel for what the unavoidable drawbacks are of utilizing RPAs to air refuel receiver RPAs?

Criteria	Likert Rating	Comments (agree/disagree/clarify)
None		
Technology development		
Reliability, consistency, and operational readiness		
Control algorithms for formation flying		

Criteria	Likert Rating	Comments (agree/disagree/clarify)
Link robustness		
Need to prevent enemy interference (anti-tamper, anti-spoofing) with the vehicle		
Lost link protocols		
Contingency management		
Hijacking risk: enemy assuming complete control of the vehicle		
High cost		
Aviator perception of RPAs		
Lack of understanding in proper employment of RPAs		
Need for an airpower practitioner to influence RPA tasking system		
Concept of operations		
Bed-down and maintenance		

5) (Programming) Please review each of the following items identified by the expert panel for what difficulties need to be addressed early in prototyping, planning, procurement, or training in order to successfully utilize RPAs as tankers to air-refuel receiver RPAs?

Criteria	Likert Rating	Comments (agree/disagree/clarify)
Interface to provide relative location data for both tanker and receiver		
Time lag in beyond line of sight scenarios		
Hand-off between beyond line of sight to line of sight data link systems		
Design-in acceptable levels of safety using common engineering practices		
Cultural challenge: pilots perceive they are "losing their jobs" to machines		
Develop prognostic health and service life surveillance to enable on-condition maintenance		

6) (All) Please review each of the following items identified by the expert panel for what paradigm shifts must occur from our current air-refueling methods to best incorporate the concept of using RPAs as tankers to air-refuel receiver RPAs, considering sound systems engineering techniques as well as the future anti-access / area denial (A2/AD) needs of tomorrow's conflicts?

Criteria	Likert Rating	Comments (agree/disagree/clarify)
Highly autonomous systems are inevitable and can protect our way of life		
American service members protect our country with less overseas basing		
Change engineering outlook to question a system from design to operation for its intended use		
Develop fully integrated system-of-systems		
Federal Aviation Administration and International Civil Aviation Authority acceptance of RPAs		
Integration of manned and unmanned flight		
Pilot acceptance of RPAs		
More emphasis on communications and security		
Safety standards must meet those of manned aircraft		
In A2/AD environment, freedom of movement must be maintained to allow for AR		
Standardized transfer method must be adaptable to and inclusive of a wide variety of platforms		
RPA AR system must allow for multiple types of fuel		
RPA AR system must allow for a wide range of potential flight profiles		

Bibliography

Adler, M. and Ziglio. E. *Gazing into the oracle: The Delphi Method and its application to social policy and public health.* London: Jessica Kingsley Publishers, 1996.

Austin, R. *Unmanned Aircraft Systems; UAVS Design, Development and Deployment.* United Kingdom: John Wiley & Sons Ltd, 2010.

Barnette, J. Likert Scaling. In N. J. Salkind (Ed.), Encyclopedia of Research Design (pp. 715-719). Thousand Oaks, CA: SAGE, 2010. Retrieved from http://sage-ereference.com/abstract/researchdesign/n219.xml.

Barnhart, R., Hottman, S., Marshall, M., and Shappee, E. *Introduction to Unmanned Aircraft Systems.* Boca Raton, FL: CRC Press, 2012.

Basom, R. *Breakaway: A Look at the Integration of Aerial Refueling and Unmanned Aircraft Systems in Future Operations.* Fort Leavenworth, KS: US Army Command and General Staff College, 1995.

Branum, D. *Capstone UAS project explores land, sea, air possibilities.* Air Force Academy Public Affairs. Retrieved from http://www.usafa.af.mil/news/story.asp?id=123297949.

Carmichael, B., Devine, T., Kaufman, R., Pence, P., and Wilcox, R. *Strikestar 2025.* Maxwell Air Force Base, AL: Air University Press, 1996.

Carifio, J., and Perla, R. *Ten common misunderstandings, misconceptions, persistent myths and urban legends about likert scales and likert response formats and their antidotes.* The Free Library, 2007. Retrieved from http://www.thefreelibrary.com/Ten%20common%20misunderstandings,%20misc onceptions,%20persistent%20myths%20and...-a0168775520.

Carreno, J., Culora, T., Galdorisi, G., and Hone, T. What's New About the AirSea Battle Concept? *U.S. Naval Institute Proceedings*, 136(8), 52-59, 2010. Retrieved from http://www.usni.org/magazines/proceedings/2010-08/whats-new-about-airsea-battle-concept.

Combat Support Branch, Air-to-Air Coordination Cell. *Future of Air-To-Air Refueling in NATO.* Kalkar, Germany: Joint Air Power Competence Centre, 2007.

Cuhls, K. *Delphi Method.* Germany: Fraunhofer Institute for Systems and Innovation Research, n.d.

Cummings, M. *Supervising Automation: Humans on the Loop.* Massachusetts: Massachusetts Institute of Technology, 2008.

Curtin, N. and Francis, P. *Unmanned aerial vehicles; Major management issues facing DOD's development and fielding efforts.* Washington DC: United States General Accounting Office, 2004.

Czinkota, M. and Ronkainen. International business and trade in the next decade: Report from a Delphi study. *Journal of International Business Studies, 28*(4), 827 – 844, 1997.

Dalkey, N. and Helmer, O. An experimental application of the Delphi Method to the use of experts. *Management Science, 9*(3), 458 – 468, 1963.

Delbeq, A., Van de Ven, A., and Gustafson, D. *Group techniques for program planning: A guide to nominal group and Delphi processes.* Glenview, USA: Scott, Foresman and Company, 1975.

Darpa completes UAV inflight refuelling demo. *Interavia Business & Technology,* (689), 27, 2007. Retrieved from http://findarticles.com/p/articles/mi_hb3126/is_689/ai_n29384726/.

Department of Defense. *FY2009-2034 Unmanned Systems Integrated Roadmap.* Washington DC: GPO, 2009.

Department of Defense. *Quadrennial Defense Review Report.* Washington DC: GPO, 2010.

Department of the Air Force, *The U.S. Air Force Remotely Piloted Aircraft and Unmanned Aerial Vehicle Strategic Vision 2005.* Washington, DC: GPO, 2005.

Dougherty, S. *Air Refueling: The Cornerstone of Global Reach – Global Power.* Maxwell Air Force Base: Air University, 1996.

Ehrhard, T. and Work, R. *Range, Persistence, Stealth, and Networking: The Case for a Carrier-Based Unmanned Aircraft.* Washington DC: Center for Strategic and Budgetary Assessments, 2008.

Eto, H. *The suitability of technology forecasting/foresight methods for decision Systems and strategy.* A Japanese view, in: Technological Forecasting and Social Change, no. 70 (2003) p. 231-249, 2003.

Ewing, P. *Navy orders study on UCLASS concepts.* 2011. Retrieved from www.dodbuzz.com.

Farrell, P. *Remotely Piloted Aircraft (RPA) Performing the Airdrop Mission.* Wright-Patterson Air Force Base, Ohio: Air Force Institute of Technology, 2010.

Fitzsimonds, J. and Mahnken, T. Military Officer Attitudes Toward UAV Adoption Exploring Institutional Impediments to Innovation. *JFQ: Joint Force Quarterly*, (46), 96-103, 2007.

Gates, R. Secretary Gates Remarks at Maxwell-Gunter AFB, Montgomery, AL. Washington DC : Federal News Service, Inc., 2008.

Griffith, P. "Seven League Boots for TAC." *The Airmen*, IV, No. 8, 44, 1960.

Harrison, T. *The New Guns Versus Butter Debate.* Washington DC: Center for Strategic and Budgetary Assessments, 2010.

Headquarters, Air Mobility Command. *Air Mobility Master Plan.* Scott AFB, IL, 2011.

Headquarters, United States Air Force. *United States Air Force Unmanned Aircraft Systems Flight Plan, 2009-2047.* Washington DC: GPO, 2009.

International Council on Systems Engineering. *What is systems engineering?* 2004. Retrieved from www.incose.org.

Jenkins, D. and Smith, T. Applying Delphi methodology in family therapy research. *Contemporary Family Therapy, 16,* 411-430, 1994.

Joint Air Power Competence Centre. *Future of air-to-air refueling in NATO.* Kalkar, Germany, 2007.

Keeney, S., Hasson, F., and McKenna, H. Consulting the oracle: Ten lessons from using the Delphi technique in nursing research. *Journal of Advanced Nursing, 53,* 205-212, 2006.

Keller, J. *Navy UCLASS program to develop carrier-based unmanned aircraft with surveillance and strike capability by 2018.* 2011. Retrieved from www.militaryaerospace.com.

Krepinivich, A. *Why AirSea Battle?* Washington DC: Center for Strategic and Budgetary Assessments, 2010.

Lauer J. and Asher J. *Composition research: Empirical designs.* New York: Oxford University Press, 1988.

Lee, C. *Embracing Autonomy; The Key to Developing a New Generation of Remotely Piloted Aircraft for Operations in Contested Air Environments.* Air & Space Power Journal, 2011. Retrieved from http://www.airpower.au.af.mil/airchronicles/apj/2011/2011-4/2011_4_06_lee.pdf.

Leedy P. and Ormond. J. *Practical Research; Planning and Design.* Upper Saddle River, NJ: Pearson Education, Inc., 2010.

Likert Scale. (n.d.). Retrieved from http://www.gifted.uconn.edu/siegle/research/instrument%20Reliability%20and%20Validity/Likert.html.

Linstone, H. and Turoff, M. (Eds.). *The Delphi Method: Techniques and Applications.* 2002. (Original work published 1975). Retrieved from http://is.njit.edu/pubs/delphibook/delphibook.pdf.

Mammarella, M., Campa, G., Napolitano, M. R., and Fravolini, M. L. *Comparison of point matching algorithms for the UAV aerial refueling problem.* Machine Vision & Applications, 21(3), 241-251, 2010. doi:10.1007/s00138-008-0149-8.

Maybury, M. *Usability in Defense Systems: Examples from Aviation.* 2011.

Mets, D. *RPAs; Revolution or Regression?* Maxwell AFB, AL: Air Force Research Institute, 2010.

Middleton, M. *Bullet background paper on automated air refueling.* N.d.

Miles, D. *Defense Leaders Laud Air-Sea Battle Concept Initiative.* American Forces Press Service, 2010. Retrieved from www.defense.gov.

North Central Texas Regional General Aviation and Heliport System Plant. *Unmanned Aircraft Systems Report.* Connecting Globally: 2011. Retrieved from http://www.nctcog.org/aa/jobs/trans/aviation/plan/UnmannedAircraftSystemsReport.pdf.

Office of the Historian. *Seventy Years of Strategic Air Refueling; 1918 – 1988, A Chronology.* Offutt AFB, NE: SAC, 1990.

Raynes, M., and Hahn, E. Building consensus using the policy Delphi method. *Policy, Politics, and Nursing Practice, 1,* 308-315, 2000.

Riconscente, M., and Romeo, I. "Technique for the Measurement of Attitudes, A". In N. J. Salkind (Ed.), Encyclopedia of Research Design (pp. 1488-1493). Thousand Oaks, CA: SAGE, 2010. Retrieved from http://sage-ereference.com/view/researchdesign/n454.xml.

Rowe, G. and Wright, G. The Delphi technique as a forecasting tool: Issues and analysis. *International Journal of Forecasting, 15*(4), 353 – 375, 1999.

Schanz, M. "The New, Responsive NRO," *Air Force Magazine,* no. 11 (November 2006). Retrieved from http://www.airforce-magazine.com/MagazineArchive/Pages/2006/November%202006/1106world.aspx.

Schmidt, R. Managing Delphi surveys using nonparametric statistical techniques. *Decision Sciences, 28*(3), 763-774, 1997.

Shaker, S. *War without men.* Washington DC: Pergamon-Brassey's International Defense Publishers, 1998.

Singer, P. Wired for War? Robots and Military Doctrine. *JFQ: Joint Force Quarterly*, (52), 104-110, 2009. Retrieved from http://www.army.mil/professionalWriting/volumes/volume7/march_2009/3_09_4.html.

Singer, P. Drones Don't Die. *Military History*, 28(2), 66-69, 2011. Retrieved from http://www.historynet.com/drones-dont-die-a-history-of-military-robotics.htm.

Skulmoski, G. and Hartman, F. The Delphi method: Researching what does not exist (yet). Proceedings of the *International Research Network on Organization by Projects, IRNOP V Conference*, Renesse, The Netherlands, 2002.

Skulmoski, G., Hartman, F., and Krahn, J. *The Delphi Method for Graduate Research.* Journal of Information Technology Education, Volume 6, 2007.

Stephenson, J. (1999). *The Air Refueling Receiver That Does Not Complain.* Maxwell Air Force Base, AL: Air University Press, 1999.

Stulberg, A. *Managing the Unmanned Revolution in the U.S. Air Force.* Elsevier Limited on behalf of Foreign Policy Research Institute, 2007.

Thompson, C. *F-16 UCAVs; A Bridge to the Future of Air Combat?* Aerospace Power Journal, 2002. Retrieved from http://www.airpower.au.af.mil/airchronicles/apj/apj00/spr00/thompson.htm.

Van Tol J. *AirSea Battle: A Point-of-Departure Operational Concept.* Washington DC: Center For Strategic and Budgetary Assessment, 2010.

Willard, R. *Prepared statement before the House Armed Services Committee on US Pacific Command Posture.* Washington DC: Senate Armed Services Committee, 2010.

Wilson, J. *A new generation of unmanned aircraft.* Aerospace America, 2007.

Woodward, M., 17th Air Force Commander. "17 AF Command Brief /CC Perspective." Address to ASAM Class of 2012. Stuttgart, Germany. 12 March 2012.

Zacharias, G. and Maybury, M. *Operating Next Generation Remotely Piloted Aircraft for Irregular Warfare.* Washington DC: Air Force Scientific Advisory Board, 2010. Retrieved from www.sab.hq.af.mil/TORs/2010/Abstract_UIW.pdf.

Zoroya, G. U.S drone operators show signs of exhaustion. 2011. Retrieved from www.usatoday.com.